4,95

Lee R Van Sickle
1969

S0-AGD-394

WOMEN
WITHOUT
MEN

WOMEN WITHOUT MEN

creative living
for singles
divorcees
and widows

DOROTHY PAYNE

PILGRIM PRESS   PHILADELPHIA   BOSTON

The author wishes to express appreciation to the individuals and publishers who granted permission to quote their materials. A list of acknowledgments is given on pages 139–40. Some of the ideas in this book were previously published in Dorothy Payne, "The Single Woman," *Pastoral Psychology* (January 1968), pages 41–47.

Library of Congress Catalog Card Number 71–94758
Copyright © 1969 United Church Press
Philadelphia, Pennsylvania

Foreword

"Yes!" is the word I want to say to this book and to its courageous author. The need for the book, and for the ministry it
illumines, deeply impresses me. For the middle-aged single
woman is massively invisible, and almost entitled to the adjectives
"forgotten" and "left-out." She is everywhere, yet nowhere. There
are virtually no ministries, secular or sacred, directed to her. She is
massive in number, yet invisible to the structures of caring in our
society.

Dorothy Payne, one of this invisible mass, does care. She has
written this book to lift the middle-aged single woman into visi-
bility. She tells her story without false modesty or varnish. She
shows the life of the American middle-aged single female *as lived*
—with all its agonies and joys, its loneliness and both real and
unreal hopes.

Dorothy Payne's life story and present ministry to unmarried
women comprise a document of Christian witness. Her primary
address, beyond the single women themselves, is to the Christian
conscience and to ecclesial institutions. But neither her Christianity nor her perspective is narrow, and those persons who
share her concern but not her faith can profit from her experience and interpretation.

Who is Dorothy Payne? She is a widowed, divorced minister
to single women on Manhattan. She may well be the only person
who is both engaged in this specialized ministry and who has a
graduate degree (Princeton Theological Seminary) in it. Dorothy
Payne is in demand as a teacher and has so served in many relationships—Protestant and Catholic and secular—including at the

Yale Divinity School Center of Continuing Education, Kirkridge, Yokefellows (Richmond, Indiana), Faith at Work, and with women's organizations in churches and groups of churches. She is also on the Consultation on Urbanization Committee, Church Women United.

If the book were written by someone other than a middle-aged single woman, it would be worth attention as pioneering in making this group of Americans visible to the larger public. If it were written by a middle-aged woman not otherwise engaged in public ministry to this group, it would have an inside feel and a plaintive quality: "Somebody ought to do something!" But the book is from the pen of one who both is of this group and is "doing something," is indeed giving her life to the concern of which she writes. I consider her the *only* one to write this book.

Part I is concerned with history, theory, and practice. The reader may want to turn first to the life story in Part II.

Willis E. Elliott
United Church Board
for Homeland Ministries

ACKNOWLEDGMENTS

The lives of my mother and my aunt are intimately bound up in the following pages. Without them this book would not have been possible. I'm also deeply indebted to Loree and Willis Elliott, Lenore Fontaine, and Milada Klatil for their long hours of research, reading, criticizing, and editing; to Elizabeth Norris, librarian at the National YWCA headquarters, for her generous help in ferreting out useful information; to the members of the Sponsoring Committee to a Ministry with Single Women for their faithful attendance at meetings and their loyal support, but especially to Agnes Forsyth, Seward Hiltner, Bruce Larson, Dr. John Oliver, and Jane Nelson, Julia Sibley, Helen Smith, and Loree and Willis Elliott, whose work and/or gifts extended beyond the meetings of the committee.

Contents

Introduction

Recently a friend said to me, "Dorothy, I don't understand the people I work for; I'm lost when I read the newspaper—in fact, it frightens me so much my inclination is not to read at all."

She, like me, is middle-aged and single. The world we knew as young girls has changed so radically and swiftly that we now live in a sort of cosmic trauma which affects us at great depth whether or not we are aware of it.

The world of our girlhood was, outwardly at least, secure. We lived in small communities with direct relationship between work and human values, and we didn't travel much. Summer vacation was an event, and the night on the town was usually a church picnic. Airplanes were a novelty, TV was not known. There were whole worlds to conquer in a Model T Ford.

Today, everything seems to be coming apart at the seams. To take only one instance of change, many women of our age and older are shocked at the sexy ads on TV, the half-naked women in the magazines and newspapers, nudity in films. We do not comprehend that the new which is beginning to emerge is bringing with it not only confusion but also challenge and invitation. Partly because the new is always strange and the strange is frightening, partly because its structure and style are still largely unperceived, we find it hard to accept—to step out with faith in it. We are anxious. What will it all mean? "Isn't it awful that the youngsters are so filthy and you can't tell the difference between the boys and the girls?" "In *my* day . . ."

How can we assume an attitude cool and courageous enough to look at changes realistically and to absorb into our consciousness the *fact* of this new style of life? There is no longer any question about its existence. What is in question is whether the middle-aged single woman—and, incidentally, the rest of the non-youthful populace—will be able to enter into creative relations with it, for the benefit of all.

Can we agree that one component of our hesitance about the new world and its life-style is our nervous nostalgia about the by-gone age? How good, we think, if we could only go back to the comfortable, secure rose bowers and wisteria-covered trellises of yesterday, where life was lived from Sunday to Sunday in a quiet, sleepy, sentimental fashion. We aren't quite sure how to act with all the "frontiers" disappearing . . . the small community a part of the past . . . cities growing larger and more impersonal all the time—the city of tomorrow extending from Boston to Washington, D.C., almost here today. The rug of the past has been torn out from under us, and we are afraid to put our feet down on the tile of the present—yet we know that if we cannot do this, we have no hope for the future.

Anxiety increases when we reflect on the fact that we scarcely know a living soul from that remote past of ours. Everyone seems to be moving somewhere, and often; and in the cities most single women live in hotels and apartment houses where the turnover of tenants is so fast that it becomes a frightening matter to try to make friends. We lose contact with both family and friends, and we more and more find ourselves in relative or almost complete isolation. On top of all this there seems no concrete way to mea-sure success, and we feel a lack of security in almost everything we do. All this is complicated by the heavy fact that we feel we must compete with men in the workaday world.

Further, those of us who, brought up in the church, seek to continue our Christian witness discover that the name of Jesus Christ is offensive and alienates many people. Our three-story uni-verse of heaven, hell, and earth no longer has meaning. The idea of earth has been transformed: we now live in one world, and Africa is as close as our TV set. Even the symbol world has shifted

—words have acquired different meanings, and new words complicate both perceiving and believing. Youth and people outside the church tend to think we are moralistic, rigid, sentimental, living in a world of unreality. They imagine we do not understand how they feel or what is going on in the world.

To make matters even worse, religion scholars disturb our peace of mind. Biblical analysts and archeologists unearth tremendous finds that should help us better understand our faith. But instead of grasping the new scholarship with hope, we tend to hide in fear that "they" are going to destroy the Bible altogether, and our faith with it. Can we no longer be sure of anything?

All this is so frightening that we try to run away into passive amusements or overwork, becoming rigid and unyielding, or perfectionistic, self-hating, and censorious. Some of us begin to treat ourselves like goddesses, indulging ourselves with too much of everything. We "spend" our lives pampering ourselves, and in doing so lose zest and spirit. Some of us seek refuge in liquor, pills, deviant ways of living, even suicide.

To all this there is a hopeful and challenging side which should help us understand something of the potential excitement of living today, in the here-and-now in which God has put us. To join the great adventure, however, we need to deal realistically, honestly, with matters as they are, not with how we might like them to be—the actual conditions in the world and in our own lives.

To begin with, let's admit it's good we're losing some of the rigid moralistic absolutes that tended to make us judgmental and prejudiced. The necessity of frequent moving is breaking down the old class structures that divided people who might otherwise have come to understand one another. The loss of the sense of history in the loss of the geographical frontier has made it harder for us Americans to tell whether we are making progress; but this can be good in teaching us to be more aware of the interpersonal frontier, the understanding of an openness to our own selves and the fellow next door.

Finally, the loss of innocence in our symbolic structures in sex, politics, and religion is forcing us to ask again what God is saying—saying to *us, today*. Is he not forcing us to live *now* by what he reveals now, and not by mindless obedience to standards tradition has set for us? This at least is what this book is suggesting, and the reader might profit from it if she has the slightest openness to this perspective.

The central concern of this book is the large number of unmarried women over thirty years of age—a group of persons almost all of whom are in the working world but otherwise virtual outsiders to the society, nurtured neither in families nor in traditional residential communities. Some of the issues we'll wrestle with are: How can we best create new images of and for the single middle-aged woman? How can we work together so that she can reconstruct her attitudes and reeducate her imagination to appropriate a sense of significance about her life? How can we awaken, expand, and furbish in her the image-making capacity which will release her into effective participation in society? How may the essence of her femininity—her femaleness—be released so that she can be the giving, loving creature she was meant to be? How can we break down two walls of prejudice which keep the single middle-aged woman locked into herself—her own prejudice against herself and her neighbor's prejudice against her?

As I was writing this book, several questions were asked me repeatedly. I want to answer these questions at the beginning so the reader may be freed to consider and respond to the central concern of this book.

Aren't you aware that in our culture the man is in a predicament if the woman is—that he, too, is threatened and frustrated by the changing roles, his own and that of the woman?

I am aware that this is true. Many men today feel a loss of power, and many would term this emasculation. Males feel insecure socially and sexually due to the increasing liberation of women, but even more from the effects of our technologized society, which threatens the male's traditional role of provider of food and therefore of life. I am in deep sympathy with the male in our culture. Only when both men and women are free from the old stereotypes and traditions will we be free indeed.

You say you're going to write a book about women without men, the single woman, the woman who is alone. Don't you realize the married woman has her problems too? She isn't free either!

Agreed! But there is a growing body of concern expressed in literature dealing with the subject of the married woman, especially the woman who is bound to "hearth and home."

On the other hand, the married woman whose family is grown may find that this book speaks to her condition in some ways that other books do not. Often, if her husband must commute or if his work causes him to travel a great deal, she is in effect a "singler."[1]

Are you trying to eliminate men altogether from the lives of single women? Where are the men in your scheme? Don't you think women should get married?

That's a whole bag of questions! No, I'm not trying to eliminate men but am trying to help the women whom our society tends to eliminate. In my scheme, men—like women—are nowhere in particular. I put them nowhere but am only concerned that persons, male and female, be free to put *themselves* wherever each can both be human and make human commitments. When you ask whether women should get married, I must respond with another question: *Which* woman? (If you had asked the same question about men, *which* man?) No, I'm not against men, but I am against whatever it is that keeps them from becoming fully male and fully human (fully "personal") in relation to women—and, in our culture, there is much that does. I affirm that whatever cripples either sex cripples both; in any culture, men and women are lost or saved *together*.

Let us, both young and old, both men and women, both married women and single women, desist from blaming one another for our present rapidly changing, roiled situation. Let's admit that the stereotypes and outmoded traditions must be either transformed or eliminated. Let's recognize that there are many forces affecting the female/male patterns and relationships today: mobility, automation, industrialization, political tension, urbanization, TV and other mass media, changing economic structures and needs, in addition to a mass lack of knowledge and understanding, and the loss of identity which results in alienation from self and others—these and many more. Once we quit blaming one another for the state we are in we can begin to bend our passions and energies toward creative transformation of our female/male relationships, whether inside or outside marriage, and our institutions and society as a whole.

part I

THE UNATTACHED
WOMAN

CHAPTER 1
The Situation

The single woman is a wider phenomenon in our nation than the black person. There are single women among every race, creed, and color. Single women are found in every hamlet, village, town, and city. Blacks of both sexes and every age make up 10 or 11 percent of the population, while single women alone over the age of thirty make up 8 to 9 percent.

In spite of similar statistics and in contrast to the black person, the single woman has scarcely been noticed. Each single woman is unique in her person and in her situation, and tends to be separate from her single sisters. This is one reason she has stayed so well hidden. Unlike the black person she has nothing visible to identify her, and her plight has not come to public awareness.

More than any other group in America, single women are marginal. On the whole, they quietly work away at boring jobs which pay less than their time and talents warrant. Of the thirty-three million women who held jobs in 1965, eight million were single, six million were widowed, separated, or divorced. A third of all these women had annual incomes of less than $3,000. Many unmarried women, out of a deep frustration, work as little as possible and do not accept full responsibility for their life. They work for the money to live, hating most of what they do. They become apathetic about social relations and bored with their dull existence.

Although there are women who live alone in apartments which they are able to make a haven of rest, a real home, other women are slowly dying spiritually and mentally because they do not have friends who visit often, and their apartment further isolates them from an already lonely life. Some women live with parents on farms, in small towns, in large cities. The reasons for living with parents vary from the childish need to stay within the safety of the womb to an adult decision to care for a parent at the end of his life. Many singles live in cubbyhole rooms in hotels; some own their own homes. Great numbers live alone while others live with an assortment of people: a female friend or friends; a brother, sister, parent(s), or other members of the family; a man. A few live in experimental communities of one type or another. With the advent of renewal among the nuns, this last situation is becoming more and more prevalent. Then there are the hippie communities, in which women are placed in the most casual kind of sharing situation.

This listing is not exhaustive, but it is sufficient to reveal the complexity of the question: where and how do these women live?

Yet while the situation of women today is complex, and single women of middle age face peculiar complexities and perplexities, at one time it was quite simple. In a single word, women's situation was *low*.

CHAPTER 2
Woman in History

The historical evidence reveals that before the time of Christ the status of women was universally low. They were given an honored place only so long as they limited themselves to the roles of wife and mother—so long as they bore children. Single women were not given any notice except in order to marry them off. Permissive polygamy was normal. The "owning" of women was one avenue of wealth: a woman was considered property, and proprietary rights rather than personal respect and love were deemed the basis of conjugal obligation. In the teachings and traditions of Jew, Greek, and Roman, and even more so in most other cultures, women were considered subordinate and inferior to men.

A characteristic feature of the second-rate place women were given in Israel is that in most cases they were not mentioned by name, even though it was through the name that one's existence and character—one's personhood—was known. Women were nothing more than a second thought—an afterthought, so to speak—easily put aside in matters of decision-making. Only the exceptional woman of the Old Testament is known by name. Most women were known as the daughter or the wife of some man.

In the time of Herod I, women did not have access to the court of the temple where the men sat, though earlier, at the Jerusalem temple and at Shiloh they had been permitted "close to the presence of Jehovah." Nor were women counted as members of the congregation; they were not allowed to read scripture, not subjected to the same ritual obligations as men nor allowed to receive religious instruction. This last point was crucial, since deprivation of religious instruction meant that women were deprived of intimate knowledge of the Law, the cornerstone of Jewish life.

Rabbi Judas Ben Elai, mid-second-century A.D., wrote: "We must every day give thanks that we are not pagan, we are not women, we are not uneducated." The good rabbi was not alone in this attitude. Many men of Old Testament times and even up to modern times have felt the same way, carrying out their feelings into actions which have resulted in keeping women in subhuman submission.

A woman was not allowed to testify in a court of law. If she did, her vow was made invalid if the father or husband did not approve.

Segregation was so complete that men felt women should not serve meals, sit at table with the guests, or even bring a message to someone at a dinner party; it was better for her to send a son to say something or ask something on her behalf.

Mothers were respected, especially for their direct influence, and occasionally a wife such as Sarah was given prominence. But to be noticed, married women had to have exceptional personalities. For the Hebrew wife was not meant to be a companion, she was meant to have children. To this end the man bought the wife from her father in much the way he would buy a slave or an animal.

Woman was prevented from realizing her inherent dignity as an image of God with inalienable rights. As long as her roles were confined to her specific functions as wife and mother, under the monopolistically male authority-figures, as long as her choice of spouse was at her family's rather than her own discretion, as long as the single state was looked on as anathema, and as long as polygamy was institutionalized, woman was prevented from realizing and developing her true identity as a person in community with freedom and responsibility for participation in society.

Against this background must be seen the accounts of Jesus talking with women and publicly counting them among his friends—

a revolutionary stance. He honored not only the mothers and wives but single women as well.

Jesus brought about the revolutionary turning point in the history of woman's status and roles. He elevated the virtues of purity, gentleness, humility, patience, care for others, love. He reestablished the divine pattern of monogamy (Genesis 2:24; Mark 10:9-12) and denied the basis for a caste system maintaining that males are superior to females (Galatians 3:26-28). The male had had complete authority in regard to the female, but the followers of Christ were admonished to be subject to one another (1 Corinthians 7:3-4). Female infanticide had been an accepted practice, but Christ declared that *children*—not designating male or female —were to be the model of adult virtue (Matthew 8:5, 10).

Where the doors of education and formal religious acceptance had formerly been closed to women, Jesus welcomed those who longed to learn from him. In the story of Jesus' relationship with Mary and Martha (two single women) we find that Mary sat at the Lord's feet and listened to his teaching. Martha did not like this because she felt she needed help preparing food and serving. When Martha said, "Lord, do you not care that my sister has left me to serve alone?" Jesus replied that Mary had chosen the good portion, which was not to be taken from her (Luke 10:38-42). Jesus not only allowed women to learn, he encouraged them to do so.

Jesus was revolutionary in his orientation toward women who were not married. Most civilizations held out no dignified alternative to women. It was marriage or no dignity at all. Jesus Christ established dedicated celibacy as a way of life. For "everyone," whether male or female, married or not married, "who has left houses or brothers or sisters or father or mother or children or lands, for my name's sake, will receive a hundredfold, and inherit eternal life (Matt. 19:29; see also Mark 10:28-30)." Jesus also maintains that it is for those who are "able to receive this," recognizing that some persons who remain single do so "for the sake of the kingdom of heaven (Matt. 19:11-12)."

Paul saluted women as well as men for their work in the church. The early monks such as Jerome gathered bands of women to assist in the translation of scriptures. So the portals of learning, teaching, and serving were opened to women as well as to men. Between the first century and today there have been numerous struggles and spurts forward in the slow process of mankind's maturation in the treatment of women.

There is a fullness of time, a time when persons are in readiness to receive a new set of values, a new way of life. Jesus opened the way, to be sure, but the world and the church were not ready to abolish the institutions centered in the male even though this way of life kept women from being full partners with men. The apostle Paul, for example, had grown up in the patriarchal atmosphere and had been educated in Hellenistic schools. It is understandable that he would be ambivalent in his attitudes toward and ideas about sexuality, women, and marriage. So the early Christian church did not overcome historic inequality of women, in spite of the fact that it tried to live communally (Acts 4:32).

Almost at once, as it happened, the teachings of Plato and Aristotle perverted those of Jesus, and the church adjusted itself to the spirit and forms of the rest of society, in which everyone knew her/his place. Communal existence was composed of patriarchs and their families, masters and slaves—the ruler and the ruled. As Violette Lindbeck said recently in a speech at Yale University, "Obedience to the powers that be—king by divine right, pope by divine succession, master by right of conquest, patriarchal father and husband by divine creation—was enjoined upon all."

But we are in a new time, a time ripe for breaking through to some of the deeper concepts of our heritage. Mutual responsibility and mutual freedom, equal opportunity, the worth and dignity of the individual, give and take rather than absolute authority, spring from attitudes which eliminate concepts like matriarchal/patriarchal and enable the "we" to emerge (see Genesis 1:26-27). Of course we need always to recognize our limitations and weaknesses, for it is these and not our strengths that enable us to give to each other and to need each other and indeed to learn responsibility for each other. These last are but a few aspects of the relationship we need to work toward, in line with Paul's vision that "there is neither Jew nor Greek, there is neither slave nor free, there is neither male nor female; for you are all one in Christ Jesus (Gal. 3:28)."

There probably will always be anger, dissension, and destructive competition where some people feel they are in and others feel they are out, where some have and others have not; but the goal of women should be to find that creative part of themselves (possibly in opportunities similar to the ones I have experienced in creative group work and dialogues), where femininity can blossom and be revealed to other women as well as to men. This femininity does not produce a subdued, chastened mouse of a person but one who in her tenderness has great strength and confidence. Such new femininity will help the world dispense with the unloving split between ins and outs, haves and have-nots.

CHAPTER 3
Social Limbo

We have always had exceptional women whose deeds and personalities have made a lasting impact on their environment and their times. Our particular historical era is marked by an effort to accept women more than ever before on an equal basis. Better health and longer life free women to look toward personal fulfillment on a new level.

Woman is on the brink of freedom from outmoded stereotypes and roles. Many women have already accepted these new freedoms and have surged forward to responsible positions in all phases of life. Large numbers of vibrant, intelligent women are moving toward active involvement, toward accepting the responsibility of decision-making which will help shape our society, toward playing their own full part in the human adventure. They are moving on the new frontiers of society as creators of the future.

Nevertheless, in our present culture, a great many unattached women in their middle years are in social limbo. Theologically, "limbo" has meant a region on the edge of hell to which are consigned the souls of the righteous who died before the coming of Christ. Generally, "limbo" means "a place of neglect or oblivion to which unwanted or worthless persons or things are relegated and forgotten; a place of confinement; a prison." Both definitions fit the feelings of millions of women who are experiencing neglect and see themselves as unwanted and forgotten. No matter how superficial their needs may seem to others, these women are in limbo.

Of those I know, most think they are alone in their plight. To assure them that they are not alone, I share below some of my findings. And to assure them (and others) that these women are needed, I appeal to them and all to meditate on the massive potential for good which has been repressed, the presently wasted capabilities that must be put to use for God's sake and man's.

The Need

Only complete isolation from the mass media of communication could keep a person unaware of the discussions and debates revolving around women today: *What is woman's role? Who is she? Is the modern woman essentially different from grandma? If so, how?* Articles, whole issues of magazines, books, radio and television programs have targeted in on young adult women (under thirty years of age), the married woman and her family, the elderly (past retirement age), and the girl on the town. But in all that has been written, said, and seen, scarcely any notice has been taken of our group, the singlers, those over forty being the most neglected. These are *forgotten people,* through no choice of their own hidden from public view.

We are a section of society which is still largely without a voice in the places where decisions are made that affect us directly and indirectly. We live in the complexities of the technological, urbanized, secular society and are dependent on that society to find meaning and purpose in life. Yet most of us are confused by it because we grew up in a very different world—a puritan rural, small-town, or suburban society. We are the largest unrecognized group in America. There is no one to lead us into the new world which is emerging around us, no one to enable us to participate fully in this world, no one sponsoring our right to a fair balance of attention, justice, and love.

Forgotten women? No choice whatsoever? Not entirely. Groups in our society—as the blacks are now proving—can struggle into the light of public attention and can minister to their internal needs. Our situation is, then, not without hope. We can help the most neglected in our own group, and we can get attention. When more persons become aware of the situation and more persons move to improve it, the singles' problems will become less agonized. We know, again from the experience in black communities, that a community in trouble tends to take responsibility for itself, but that in order to do so it must have the proper tools. So too with the single woman. She needs to be awakened to the resources for facing her situation creatively; then she will want to awaken others. Awakened, our group can and will move together toward a society more just for all.

Cold statistics translate out into flesh and blood, and it is with the flesh and blood that this book is concerned.

Item: In the United States, according to the 1960 census, there were 41,109,763 unmarried people of marital age. Of this total, 12,380,049 were single women; another 10 million were widowed or divorced. Others, for whom there are not proper statistics, were separated. Of the 12 million single women, nearly half were in their middle years. In Chicago, in one area of 10 census tracts where high-rise apartments account for 70 percent or more of the population, live 56,873 souls. Forty-one percent of this group is listed as unrelated individuals. The median age is about 45, and the number of women is nearly a third greater than the number of men. Average adult education is nearly two years of college. One church survey declares that there are 20,000 single women in one small area just east of the Drake Hotel in San Francisco, living together in tiny rooms, often with not enough to eat.

Item: Eight percent of the men and 7 percent of the women in the United States over the age of 30 are unmarried.

Item: Many of these women have left homes and parental families because they have been, or at least have felt, rejected. Several million are to be found, particularly in large cities, adrift, lonely, and often desperate. Most have church roots but have found that the church, too, has rejected or at least neglected them and is now scarcely aware of their existence.

Item: Woman's life-span in the United States is now 76 years. If we consider her youth as 20 and that her desire and hope to marry take most of her spare time to the age of 30, she has remaining to her 46 years. During this time neither our society nor our churches do anything significant to provide a meaningful community in which the single person can find herself in association with others and in service.

Item: Ninety percent of our population in the near future will live in large urban complexes where a lone woman will get lost in the crowd.

Item: The United States Population Profile reported that there were nearly 1,000,000 more 17-year-olds in 1964 than in 1963, and that each succeeding crop of 17-year-olds will be larger than the one before. This poses a growing problem with the middle-aged in years to come, to say nothing of the elderly which the present middle-aged will become.

Item: Many singles have nothing more hopeful on their horizon than the deplorable conditions of the present elderly. When days of retirement come for the singler who is without home and family, what then? In a very few years this situation will create a social problem of the aged which far surpasses what we know today. One woman I know who works with a large social agency concerned with the elderly and their plight said to me, "When I'm forced to speak to women in their middle years, I have no hope to offer them for the future. They must begin now to create a better world for themselves if they don't want to get caught in this trap."

Women today are searching for a new identity which will suit the new sociocultural patterns which have risen around them and which are shaking the ancient foundations. The married women seem to be on a more active search, but all women everywhere want to know what this new world we are coming into is about and what woman's role in it is to be.

The majority of women seem to be asking, "How can we achieve equality with men (in job opportunities, wages, education)?" or "How can I find fulfillment?" I would like them to ask two different questions: *What does our society need most that women can supply?* and *How can I best fulfill my destiny?*

Our world needs most women who have learned to listen and to love, women who can call others out of the prison of the self into life here and now. Woman fulfills her destiny as woman-person in doing just that. To put it symbolically, woman, any woman, fulfills her destiny by allowing herself to become pregnant with the pains of the world, bringing to birth the spirit of Christ within herself. Any woman, married or single, young or old, can be bride, spouse, mother in the highest sense of the words. Mankind needs you to assume these roles in an open, wholesome, free manner.

If woman is to fulfill her destiny in this way, she must come to know what the most essential elements of life are. It seems to me that these essentials are love, joy, and peace, and that there is a deep longing in most persons for these fruits of the Spirit. Persons may be misguided in how to achieve these fruits, but this is what each one desires.

I've never heard a nervous, depressed, anxious woman say she wanted to be nervous, depressed, and anxious. Her cry is usually, "How can I find peace? What can I do to relax and be at home with myself and my world?"

I've never heard an angry, bitter woman say, "I enjoy being this way. I like to be bitter and angry." They say they must be hostile to cope with life and people. But when their guard is down, they become honest and say, "My real problem is that I don't know how to love anyone, least of all myself." Even more difficult to face than the knowledge that one is not loved is that one *cannot* love. In fact, inability to love prevents one from feeling the love that is, in actuality, available to us—not being able to *give* love is the other side of not being able to *receive* it.

I have yet to hear a sad, despairing, humorless person say she was happy. Every unhappy woman who has ever spoken with me deeply has revealed her yearning for joy and laughter and fun.

Being overserious they cry, "Why is all life so serious and problem-laden? Why am I?"

True womanhood is a mystery—a mystery of which we have scarcely touched the hem. We need to do everything within our knowledge and power to bring forth in flesh and blood terms what it really means to be a woman in this latter part of the twentieth century. Those who are not involved in the emergence of this new womanhood may not believe that there is more to being a woman than just being or just existing, and they may not understand what all the noise is about. But it is important that each woman learn to ask the proper questions about herself in relation to being a person and to being a woman-person.

Father Franc Prokes, Jesuit professor at the University of Detroit, maintains that within five years a university will not be "with it"—will not have the proper status—unless it has departments of religion and theology whose professors will be both men and women. The universities that are informed in this regard, he says, are already asking for women doctoral theologians five years in advance. But we have very few women theologians. Nor do we have very many females who have grown to know what their destiny as women is. It is not enough for a woman to be a mathematician, a politician, a historian, a clerk, a typist, says Father Prokes. She must be in mathematics as a woman, in politics as a woman, a historian as a woman, a clerk or typist as a woman. For too long we have neglected the female element in all areas of life, and only woman can find the way to return it to the world.

An intense, domineering, harsh female comes across to others like a man in a woman's body. She is not fulfilling her feminine and human potential, and this is the crux of her problem. We women do not have to act like men in order to find our niche in the twentieth century. The world needs women, not men in women's bodies.

Have we women sold our birthright for a mess of pottage? As though famished as Esau was, are we obsessed with equal rights, equal pay, better business and educational opportunities, and missing the birthright? Of course we need to be whole persons, and part of being whole comes from being treated with respect and justice. Of course a great deal needs to be done to destroy the subtle and terrible barriers that exist between men and women. But I believe woman is looking in the wrong place for fulfillment. Men have run the world for so long that women now are following in men's footsteps at those points where women finally do get out into the world.

Woman has her bowl of pottage, but she is still hungry. She may need to go to Jabbok (a river of living water) and wrestle till the break of day (awareness) with the Spirit of light and love until that Spirit blesses her (Genesis 32:22-30). With new vision and courage, she needs to seek for the best ways to bear the fruits of the Spirit: love, joy, peace, patience, kindness, goodness, faithfulness, gentleness, self-control. If she does not come to bear these fruits, she will come to hate her birthright as surely as Esau hated his. She will not have lived a full life of adventure and joy. She will not have fulfilled her potential. She will not have become truly woman, or person. She will not have received, as Jacob did, a new name and personality. She will still be in limbo.

Our society has had enough of the masculine, aggressive thrust. This competitive activism desperately needs to be diverted to a more humane way of thinking and living. We need to counter the technological society man has created for us with feminine patience and compassion.

However we may view the virgin birth its meaning includes this, that Mary, a single woman, gave birth to Jesus. She was given the honor of presenting Christ in the flesh.

Mothers who bear children physically have a specific privilege in that they have the satisfaction which comes from the physical nearness of the fetus in the womb, and from the pain and releasing joy during childbirth itself. Single women can experience this great miracle and mystery only vicariously. But any woman, regardless of her state in life can, with love, bring forth the spirit of Christ. What if only a few of the twelve million single women in America decided to take seriously the injunction to "love the Lord your God with all your heart, and with all your soul, and with all your mind, and with all your strength," as well as the second injunction, "Love your neighbor as yourself (Mark 12:30, 31)"? What if only a few women decided that love without overt sex just might work?

What would it mean for us women to call one another into the fullness of life here and now? To enable one another to fulfill our individual potentials for creativity and involvement?

What are the possibilities of interrelatedness between married women and single women? between young single women and older single women? between married couples and single people? between persons in an old people's home and other institutions of like nature and those of us who are "free"? between the women of the suburbs and those of the city? between men of all ages and women of all ages? between the little child and the older woman?

Is there something women have to say to our world today that, at this point in the world's pilgrimage, no one else can say? If so, what is it? What is the best way we can say it?

Are there matters of significance which woman needs to convey and which the world needs to hear that will help bring in a celebrative sense of existence and advance both the dignity and fulfillment of each and the welfare of all?

CHAPTER 4

Woman's Image

As sex is taken less seriously, as single women themselves live more fruitful lives, and as our married sisters fight for liberation, fewer and fewer jokes are made about the single woman. Still, society's censure of singleness, and therefore of the singler, is powerful and cruel: society's ideal is that a woman should be married and bear children. Woman is seen not as an individual but as a class. M. D. Hugen says:

> Although the single woman is a social problem surrounded by prejudice and taboo, she is not considered a sufficiently dignified subject for academic research. At very best, society's attitude to the single woman is one of condescending pity, . . . as a handicapped person, to be classified with the cripple and the deformed.[1]

The woman of today often bears little resemblance to the retained images of her Victorian grandmother. Education, work outside the home, travel, new types of responsibility have helped to mature her and give her new capabilities, longings, ambitions. Madeleine Barot says that in spite of this "she is still inhibited by the weight of tradition and crushed by the multiple roles that the present period of transition lays upon her." [2] She wants to be free of the prejudices and the minority position placed upon her, but she does not know how to become free.

Probably the fundamental problems of the single woman are her aloneness and her facelessness. These become deep-rooted spiritual problems which are intensified by the social isolation into which our culture forces her. Any deep relationship she does have is suspect, since it is with her own sex. As Hugen says of such women, "They miss much of that communion of believers which is necessary for the building up of faith and love. They commonly feel a lack of purpose and any sense of life because of their detachment from society." [3]

The singler's isolation is increased in American culture by the breakdown of clan living, by urbanization and mobility, by the social opprobrium of singleness, and by the lack of regular contact on a personal level. "Even if the single woman is ready to join society as an active member, if society refuses to accept her because of its stereotyped judgment of the unmarried, she may, through her isolation, become what society thinks she is." [4]

What about her social life? She is an outsider almost everywhere she goes, and more often than not her efforts to find companionship intensify the limbo-state in which she is trapped. For example, a cruise for "singles only" had 300 women and only eleven men; an "introduction bureau" introduced the same handsome man to at least fifteen widows whom he saw singly and in groups; a "marriage broker" service worked up just one marriage in a full year, while it collected regular fees from hundreds of hopefuls.

What are some of the other ways in which society condemns the individual single middle-aged woman to a dehumanizing life of loneliness and impotence?

She is virtually ignored in all media of communication; by her family, who want her married and off their conscience; by the church, which has allied itself almost exclusively with the concerns of the family.

She usually works at a job which bores her and which is itself depersonalizing. Seldom does she have the opportunity to use her own initiative. Even if she is a private secretary, if the boss uses machines for dictation and other forms of communication she identifies with the machine instead of with him. Harold M. Schmeck recently reported: "Modern mechanized society may unintentionally have made American women the loneliest, hardest-working, most isolated women who have ever lived." [5] Even the rare professional woman who may use initiative is not allowed to bring the uniqueness of her femininity to the job.

Thus the single woman has feelings of impotence before the powerful and those who manipulate and exploit. Probably nowhere else in the world has loneliness been capitalized on for profit as it has been in America's largest cities, which have the highest concentrations of single women. Younger women especially get caught up in the lure of finding men at resorts, on cruises, and at bars and parties. They are humiliated by the generally poor quality in the media of movies, television, magazines, books, which stimulate nothing in them to encourage persistence in the search for meaning and in growth toward maturity. The only choice offered them is the emptiness of conformity. The mass media simply do not speak to their condition.

Almost always what the single woman wants to do is separated from her making a living. This leads to a *contradiction* that undermines her self-respect, her enjoyment of what she does most of the time, and her sense that there is meaning in life. Her values become twisted and unworthy of her true capabilities.

Even the names we call her are dehumanizing; they range from derogatory to degrading. "Middle-aged single" does not concede that she is in the prime of life. "Single" connotes young adult (before thirty) and implies that she is without something. "Old maid" and "spinster" are fortunately going out of style along with some other stereotypes. "Manless," yes, but would you call a single man "womanless?" "Bachelor girl" has the odor of someone "on the town," which few women in this group are. "Celibate?" No, for she probably has not chosen her singleness as a vocation, especially if she is Protestant. We do not help women to make this choice.

In an age that flaunts and inflates qualifications for marriage, "the single woman is seen as a sexual failure as well as a personal failure. She is not seen as an individual but as a class." [6] If the woman is a virgin, society labels her virginity as the cause of her oddness, "for the single woman is always seen as lacking the qualities necessary for the pattern of marriage in our age. Marriage is considered such a central and important obligation of woman in our culture that it has become the primary purpose of her existence" [7]—her god. One result is that thousands of American women are placing their bodies on the auction blocks of resorts all over the world in the hope of snaring a man. These forays damage ego identity, and scarcely ever serve their purpose.

Protestantism, because of its reaction against the monastic ideal, has made the unmarried state contemptible. Where marriage and motherhood are viewed as woman's ultimate purpose, the older unmarried woman is viewed, automatically, as a failure, a faulted human being.

The prejudgment of society operates precisely like any prejudice. "It may be as difficult to show that one's singleness is not necessarily neurotic as it is to demonstrate that another's dark pigmentation does not necessarily make him [her] stupid." [8]

Results of Individual and Social Inadequacy

What happens when our faceless woman is pushed to the limit by both social rejection and her own inadequacy to meet the situation or to find help for it? She may turn to various forms of addiction, masturbation, homosexuality, even suicide.

The following examples of disintegration are extreme cases, to be sure, and are among the minority of our minority. Still, if we are to face the issue of the single woman we must be aware of all facets of the situation. These findings are particularly relevant in light of the fact that each of these outer manifestations of inadequately dealt with inner conflicts is multiplying at a startling rate.

I have lived in a woman's hotel in Manhattan, have visited friends living in similar hotels and sat in the lobbies of them. I have talked with hundreds of women and have had dialogue at

some depth with more than forty in the past four years. My findings are in line with the statistics.

SUICIDE

Americans are destroying themselves at the rate of fifty per day
(one every twenty-six minutes). Many of the women I have
talked with have thought about suicide at some point in their life
as a solution to their loneliness. Feeling cast aside, having no con-
vincing reason to live, their reason sometimes urges them to destroy their life.

Many middle-aged women fall into self-destructive patterns at
menopause which add to the already heavy load of unresolved
problems. When they talk about suicide, they are crying out for
some kind of releasing communication.

ILLNESSES

Some unmarried women (and married women as well) use illness—real or imagined—to withdraw from life. There is much
genuine physical suffering among women, and I do not want to
appear indifferent to it. But *pain itself can be redemptive.* When
one is able to give oneself over to the pain without fear of what
the outcome will be, healing of some sort takes place. At times
it may be an actual physical healing. At others it might appear
in a new mood, in which a person is so grateful to be alive that
grass looks like emeralds and leaves like diamonds, the air seems
especially exhilarating, and there is greater sensitivity to sound
and odor.

Yet again, the release from pain may result in an insight into
some way you are deceiving yourself, belittling yourself, or running from life. Then you are set on a new course if you accept
the challenge of healing in your attitudes. A day of enforced rest
may be the needed ingredient to bring about an awareness of some
specific thing you can do to mend a relationship, renew a friendship, or in some manner move out to others in a more whole-
hearted way than formerly. One of these or some other kind of

healing will come, of this I am convinced, if you are willing to accept *the pain as part of the learning process.*

ADDICTION

Sleeping pills, tranquilizers, pep pills, alcohol, and religion are the five most severe addictions among women I know.

Drugs. The drug problem is complicated by the fact that the vast majority of users of non-narcotic drugs first obtained these through the prescription of a physician—a fact which gives vague, though irrational, sanction to the addiction. Doctors first administer the drug to "calm" and "cheer" the patient. This only drives the energy (anxiety) inward, causing great loss of creativity—a chemical dulling if not deadening of imaginative and critical capacities. Often the persons who finally succumb to drugs and alcohol are sensitive, imaginative, thoughtful persons who have been unable to balance the dichotomies and paradoxes of life as they have known it. Once they are allowed to pass through the pain of confronting themselves and "kicking" whatever habit has them in its grip, they can become creative creatures once again. But they need a loving person—better still, a loving community, standing by while they go through the fire.

The woman who habitually takes pills may do so for many reasons, but the ultimate outcome will be the same: she will not be fulfilling her potential as a person and therefore will eventually be troubled by many physical problems she might otherwise have avoided. There are times, of course, when pills are necessary. I am only saying that our culture is pill-sated and most pill-taking deters the true health that is able to make all things whole and new. Thus the pill-taker may be using chemistry to add fuel to the fire of her frustrations and resentments. Of course not all who leave off pills will be healthy.

Persons are too complex for simplistic prediction. Beyond their educational and redemptive values is yet mystery in pain and suffering. I plead that we give this mystery more of an opportunity to work its graciousness in our lives.

Alcohol. It has been estimated that there are approximately nine secret alcoholics for every one under treatment. Most of the women who admit drinking say they started it as a way of forgetting the loneliness, of blunting the pain of reality. Alcoholism climbs at a steep 50 percent in the forty-sixty age group over the thirty-forty age group. However, as with drugs, what begins as a desire for personal well-being and protection against life ends in a paralysis of will for every waking action.

Religion. If addiction is a habit, a constant practice to which we resort to escape reality, then religion for thousands of women, as it is taught and understood, can be termed an addiction. James E. Loder has indicated that much of present-day religion is "pathological religiousness." He says:

> The intrapsychic pain or tension created by the inability to bear how things "seem" to be (the anxiety or despair is too great) and the seemingly necessary falsification of what "is" lead to the creation of *illusory* views of the world or *delusional* interpretations of it. Both are attempts to find "meaning" in the pain or "a meaning" behind the pain.[9]

Often pastors are unwitting administrators of this palliative.

HOMOSEXUALITY

Among the women I have talked with there were only four who admitted to overt homosexual behavior (though verbal admissions do not reflect the extent of the practice). One had been so overcome by revulsion and fear after one "engagement" with another woman that she withdrew completely from the little social life she did have with other women. Another, after a great deal of conversation, sought clinical help and was later married. Many others said they were confused by current new attitudes; and several were, or had been, forced to work through their feelings after the shock of being approached by a lesbian. Still other women have tendencies in this direction, but are not at all aware of their condition.[10]

The important point here is that much of the pain and conflict could have been avoided had these women had a qualified counselor with whom they could talk. An accepting group is also a good agent of wholeness providing there are experienced persons present. There must be outlets where women can feel secure in being open and honest about their problems.

MASTURBATION

Her revulsion for herself and her condition, especially for the middle-aged and older woman who grew up in puritan surroundings, is so great that masturbation is the last thing a woman wants to discuss, even with another woman. The middle-aged woman today was born and grew up in a time when masturbation was considered wicked, depraved, even dangerous. She does not realize she is one of the 60 percent of women who engage in this activity. She suffers mental turmoil because of her sense of guilt; she feels "dirty" and perverse.[11]

Due to lack of dialogue, especially on deep-seated matters, she often has little insight into her general condition. She is not aware that her revulsion is not just with the act of masturbation itself but with her whole life. The SIECUS (Sex Information and Education Council of the United States) Study Guide #3 says:

> Masturbation . . . can . . . be a symptom of many nonsexual conflicts. Boredom, frustration, loneliness, a poor self-image, inadequate . . . relationships, conflict with parents, too many pressures. . . . It is not the masturbation that should be treated by suitable counseling but the conflict of which it is a symptom.[12]

SEX VIOLATIONS

An appalling number of women have been violated by a man before the age of ten—usually by someone within the child's own family: a brother, an uncle, a cousin, less often a father. These women almost never discussed this with anyone as a child, especially not with their mothers. The humiliation lay within like a raw cancer eating away dignity and worth, even the desire to live. A report in the *Saturday Evening Post* revealed: "For a special study John Gagnon . . . interviewed 4,500 women. Twenty-five percent, he discovered, had been subjected at some time between the ages of 4 and 13 to one of a variety of sexual experiences from exhibitionism to direct contact." [13]

The United States Children's Bureau says that in 83 percent of the cases they interviewed, the offender against a child was a member of the child's own environment. One out of four offenses was incest.

The common factor in each of these problems is lack of communication: absence of people of primary importance in one's life who make an effort to understand or care. I want to stress that most of these women are intelligent, talented, often artistic persons. All of them maintain steady jobs in reputable companies. The prejudgments of society and their environmental isolation have been responsible for many psychological or emotional problems.

A View from Within

How do such women feel? What is their inner climate in their aloneness?

The following remarks are from *letters and conversations* I have had with other single middle-aged women. I have chosen them as apt expressions of my own experience of having once been in social limbo.

·   ·   ·

Life is a forlorn hell. My world consists of a single room, park benches when it's warm, cafeteria solitude, long nights interrupted only by the footsteps going by my door or coughing from some room down the hall. I mean nothing to anyone, therefore I am nothing.

•   •   •

One woman who lives in a hotel with 350 other women said, "I'm so alone that if anything happened to me, it would be days before anyone would know."

•   •   •

How I have longed for a group where I can get out of the hell of me, myself, and I! I've searched this city north, east, south, and west and have found no group which will allow me to dig into the real issues of life or be myself. No one even seems to want your services. Now I'm resigned—too beat, too dead.

•   •   •

Surrounded as I am by steel, stone, and electricity, I sometimes think I am become like them—hard, unfeeling, perhaps brilliant at times—and sweeping to the skies for something unobtainable.

•   •   •

Oh, sure, we professional women are considered to lead full lives. No one ever asks what we do after our long hours of hard work with its impersonal associations. We try to find inner meaning in life by attending plays, concerts, and the like, but we return to our lonely rooms and apartments unfulfilled, lonely, dreading the emptiness and aloneness we will feel once the door is shut. Many nights I literally run from this apartment for fear I will do something drastic if I remain one more moment alone. I go to sit alone in a restaurant because at least there are bodies there. Some of those bodies are in love and others in other states of being together. But they *are* together, and that increases my pain. At last, weary to the bone, I return to my apartment and sleep in sheer exhaustion. I was an alcoholic, you know. Afterward, it took all my strength and will power not to go to the nearest bar. Many times I wonder why I don't, and whether I will succumb again under the oppressive weight of this awful loneliness. It is agony.

•   •   •

The mass of women in their middle years are neither free nor welcome in mixed companies—except as servants or audiences.

.   .   .

After a few years of being cast aside you begin to feel uneasy, unworthy, defeated, bored, isolated, just plain sick. Sick with yourself and with a life which holds nothing but meaninglessness.

.   .   .

How does it feel to be alone at forty? Hostile! This is a man's world!

.   .   .

Sometimes the loneliness is so bad you count heavily on no more than just friendly looks and react exaggeratedly to signs of disfavor of any kind.

.   .   .

A woman who lives in a woman's hotel and works among women says, "Sometimes the very appearance of a man in the lounge causes vibrations of shock."

.   .   .

Another woman who has just recently moved to a woman's hotel said with dismay: "They look at TV in unkempt little rooms. They come out all frowsy and cook little messes in pots—and take it to their rooms where they eat it alone. You can tell they aren't slummy people—just have nothing to live for and are all alone. They look sad and pathetic, everyone staying in her little center of isolation and private chaos."

.   .   .

I've been alone so long that I feel like a ghost: being present but not really in contact with anyone.

.   .   .

If the devil does not abide in me, who does? Or am I an empty vessel? Oh, I put up a front and get along, but surely God cannot exist in someone whom no one wants or loves? How do you learn to live in relationship with others?

.   .   .

My more elemental needs are buried, except when manifested by overeating, because the church concerns itself so much with doctrine. I feel that when these matters do occupy the mind they should be thrashed out; they are valid causes for both good and bad emotions—even hatred. Where can we get help for understanding these dichotomies? Especially people like me, whose hope hangs on Christ's forgiving love—which I have not yet felt?

•   •   •

All the different branches of Christianity I have tasted have done nothing to give me a *knowing* feeling of God's love, though many have given me a glimpse of God's truth, yet without conviction. How I yearn to know God's love! Can you help me? What sense is there to this mortal existence when there is warmth from neither God nor man?

•   •   •

Daily I seem to lose power, not only as a person but as a mind, in my lonely existence. One needs companions for conversation to stretch the mind and spirit. I desperately need the *physical* presence Bonhoeffer talks about, especially of other Christians, for I find I cannot be a Christian or a person alone. And in this impersonal city, whether at work, eating, play, or in my hotel, people are not even aware that I exist.

•   •   •

I was so despairingly alone that it was impossible to grasp the messages from the pulpit about love and compassion and healing.

Long ago I learned that the churches are for the old and the young and for cozy little families. Without knowing love or feeling any sense of grace to uphold you, it is not easy to believe that God loves you or that he wishes to prepare you for some service. Too much being alone just doesn't give you the sense of being cared for. It isn't that you consciously seek rewards first, but that you want reassurance that you're heard and wanted. When you're not, it can make you feel downright mean.

•   •   •

It seems to me that in the churches and social agencies to which I've gone to try to be more with people, the atmosphere is so proper and genteel that nobody would dream of admitting it if they were alcoholic or suicidal. I *know* that's true, for I could not admit my pill-taking (barbiturates) today though I long desperately to be rid of this killing habit. Where can I go for help without a million dollars?

·   ·   ·

Once in the golden morning
I wandered far from town,
Where orchards were in blossom
And petals drifted down.

And I was drenched in glory.
The roads were hot and white.
Pebbles shone bright as money,
And sands were jewel-bright.

And what I met were prophets
With faces stern and wise.
A brightness like a heaven
Lit my exulting eyes.

Now it is later—later,
I wander toward the town.
Dim in the gathering twilight
The leaves are shaken down.

And dim are the shapes of people
Hurrying to and fro.
Lord of the Holy Answers,
Where did the brightness go?

·   ·   ·

It is just to expect more from the church than from other organizations, yet the church has been dragging its heels in the matter of the single person as it has in other aspects of modern life. The church in America calls itself a family church and all its activities and services revolve around the family even when the church is in an area where there are more single people than families. This condition makes it difficult for the single person to feel accepted, let alone loved. Thus most single women seldom go to church; they no longer trust the church to be a forgiving and accepting community.

Trust is fundamental to the understanding of one's own identity and the developing of faith in God's love and mercy. This makes it mandatory for the church to create a climate of trust, so that single women can be drawn into the Christian fellowship. If the church were to treat single women as human beings it would discover a powerhouse of talent and service which is now going to waste.

A pastor friend who has many middle-aged single women in his parish is deeply concerned about their welfare. He recognizes their exterior and interior situation and says, "How can I raise the subject of developing the potential of the single woman in her presence and keep her from panicking? When I try to discuss your proposal with those for whom it is designed, their reaction is that of impalas who have just heard a shot fired. I remember your saying a man can't do much at this point—it takes women trained to listen. Tell me how one introduces the subject to those who need to hear about it."

This, of course, is one of the greatest difficulties. Our success-god will not allow us to fail; our youth-god will not allow us to grow old; our fear of death will not allow us to begin to live in the here and now. But it is up to the church to find a way. It is not an easy task. As with any social problem, we need to take a long look at the reality of the situation. Then we must turn our knowledge and educational facilities to creating adequate images, models, and experiences to enable the wounded ones to ask the right questions and to work for the right answers through developing their own potential.

CHAPTER 5

Running After Jesus

I have seen women in a psychiatric ward of a clinic whom I felt were living in a cavern, dumb with grief, closed possibly forever from life and the use of their own unique gifts and potentialities. Many times I've wondered to what extent we fail them in not just sitting quietly in prayer for them, calling them out of themselves by energizing love.

On the other side of the walls that separate us from the psychiatric wards are women with whom I converse daily, who lead active lives in offices during the day but who live in a lonely apartment or a cell of a room where, though they be without attendants or nurses, they are like their institutionalized sisters. We have withheld our prayers and our love too long to be effective with some who are locked away by law, but it is not too late to reach the human beings who still have the freedom to possess their own keys to their own bleak and empty rooms.

So many single women I know are caught, as I was, in the box of disdain for the self. They become so used to consciously and unconsciously berating themselves and their lot in life, to feeling unloved and unwanted, that they become actually untouchable and unlovable.

Often it is the church woman who feels most this way. For years we have heard from pulpits what sinners we are, how easy it is to fall into sin, how difficult it is to be good and pure and holy. When we were told about kindness, joy, patience, gentleness, it was in a manner which seemed to imply that to attain to these great virtues was a mammoth feat, indeed impossible, because all is dependent on God. But if we don't feel God loves or cares, where is the hope? We are lost in a mire of mud and filth from which we feel powerless to extricate ourselves.

Love enters in the form of understanding and says that there's a hopeful way to look at all life. One can make a choice *for* life rather than *against* it.

Each unique person finds fulfillment in her own way. Each road is individual. But I found mine by attempting to live in the spirit of Christ. Through study, confrontation with one another (one friend and I first, and later others), and prayer, I was slowly enabled to choose life. At one point I made a study of the fruits of the Spirit and recognized that the more I thought about them the more I wanted these vital, energizing qualities. The more I wanted spiritual values, the more readily they seemed to become available to me. Some of the thoughts I had in those days I share here so that you may compare them with the negative choices mentioned in chapter 4.

The fruits of the Spirit listed in Galatians 5:22-23 are love, joy, peace, patience, kindness, goodness, faithfulness, gentleness, self-control. In Ephesians 4:1-3 Paul says that life in the Spirit (of love) helps us to forbear one another in love, makes us eager to maintain unity in bonds of peace. In such a spirit we are more liable to speak the truth (to be honest and open), to be tender-hearted, forgiving, and thankful; and when we are angry we will not sin by holding it in our hearts. In Romans 12:9-21 this celebrative way of life includes rejoicing in our hope, holding fast to what is good, dispensing with conceit, weeping with those who weep, and rejoicing with those who rejoice. These involve choices toward living life to the full in the present. Later I came to recognize these as the essential ingredients of true womanhood and true manhood.

I recall a specific instance that led me to search out these fruits of the Spirit. Loree Elliott and I were conversing, and I was castigating myself as I complained to her that no one could possibly love me. She replied, "Don't worry about what other people think or say. Their attitudes can't hurt you. It is your forgiving attitude toward them which is necessary for God's forgiveness to happen for you. If you think about hate and resent the expression of it in others, you encourage its growth. It can only be erased by wholesome thoughts. This attitude is not as easy to achieve as it is to explain. But at least you know who your real enemy is, and that's half the battle."

In much the same way, as long as I thought about how domineering I was and hated myself for being so rigid and fearful, the more so I became. Now I turned my mind toward hope in gentleness. What makes me ungentle? I wondered. If I have a heavy crust of hardness around me, no one can get into me— I cannot be in union or communion with others. All the great people I know, women and men, are gentle and tender. They are approachable. They enter into you, into your pains and your joys. You feel loved, accepted. How can one change? By beginning to think gently and live gently.

What we choose begets more of what we have chosen. If I choose to be thankful and turn myself toward gratitude, I soon discover that there are more and more things to be happy about. As soon as I choose to turn my mind toward the things I do not have, I accumulate many things about which I'm ungrateful.

Rather than despising myself for the hostility in my heart, I turned my thoughts away from this unhealthy (sinful, unfruitful) pursuit to considering what it really meant to live a life of love and loyalty. I discovered that in simply turning from the old to ask questions about the new I was forced to make new choices. It became necessary for me to discover and use another fruit of the Spirit, self-control, to bring the emotions of resentment to bay. Why did I feel anger, anyway? What could I do to be free of this burden and love loyally? This was my responsibility.

I learned quite quickly that you can live with any of the unhealthy qualities all your life through fear or self-deceit. Yet if you do, you die. Your body may live on, but *you* die. Like a tree you may become rigid and petrified or, like a sad rag, limp and lifeless. The essential *you* is dead. Dead as a stone.

As I look back I cannot maintain that the road to choosing life rather than death is easy and free of hurdles, but I've learned that if you wish to live fully and richly, vitally and adventurously, you can. Age makes no difference; years are swept away in the adventure. This is the new life Christ offers; the choice is ours.

Idolatry was and remains a tricky negative quality. We worship so much in this life other than God. We worship everything from clothes and cars and travel to persons and ideals, youth, marriage, children—and even the gifts of the Spirit! This was brought forcibly home to me during a retreat. The leader asked us to sit quietly for ten minutes and reflect upon the most important thing, event, person, or place in our life. It did not matter at all what this was. But during the ten minutes, if there was more than one thing, we were to sift and sort until we came to *one* which stood out clearly and completely from all else.

In the first few seconds dozens of pictures crossed my mind. Quite rapidly they were resolved to a specific act of love toward me on the part of a human being. But why did this specific act stand out as Number One? It was Christ I wanted to be Number One. What did this mean? This particular act of love had, more than any other act of love, welded together all the others in such a way that it pointed me toward an inner understanding of Jesus' love for me. In the end, then, it was Jesus' love which had been manifested through the best tool he has available—a human being. So which was most important: the persons who had pointed me to Christ, the acts of love, or Christ himself whom I could not have known without the lesser love? I finally decided that I must choose Christ himself; there was no other choice. He would never go away or die or remove his presence from me; thus love would always be available. But, even so, I could not completely separate him from myself and my neighbor who had loved. At that moment in the reverie, joy unasked flooded my being. I was at peace. My choice seemed right. Shortly after, the leader's voice interrupted the silence. "Do not tell me what your choice has been," said he. "Let it teach you. For whatever you have named, this is your present God."

Life did not begin for me at birth, when I got my first job, or at forty. It began when I wholeheartedly turned my attention to running after Jesus Christ, to feasting on his every word and action. I know it is not "in" to talk about God, and "running after Jesus" sounds downright Freudian! Fear that my secular friends would scoff almost made me leave out this section of the book.

But conviction is growing in me that not only our youth but all of us are sick of how-to's and you-ought-to's. We've had enough of words without experience and theory without testimony. One reason people don't want to hear God's name anymore is that we Christians have mouthed the pious words "God loves" so long without ourselves showing love to persons who need it that our actions belie our words. Our words become a lie—a blatant desecration. And so people say, "Be still! I don't want to hear about your God any longer. *Show* me his love and I may be interested; *show* me his power and I may pay attention."

We have also had enough of an intellectualism about God and religion which lures us on and on but never satisfies even so much as our brains.

All of us thirst and hunger for the experiences which can come only through our attention to Jesus Christ: the experiences of communion, peace, love, joy—and we are increasingly impatient with substitutes.

Al Carmines of Judson Memorial Church in New York City said in a sermon recently, "Old Simeon in the temple had prayed and had theologized all his life till he was an old man. But when he saw the Child he gave way to experience." Like Simeon we all long that our eyes *see* our salvation. We want to taste, feel, touch, experience the divine. We have limited interest in discussing religion; we want to find an authentic experience of the person of Christ for ourselves.

I believe this deeper hunger explains why many of us are getting fed up with personalism as manifested in all kinds of groups: sensitivity training groups, talk-it-over groups, therapy groups, marathons, dialogue groups—all groups that hold out a promise of openness, love, and liberation from anxiety. These, for many, pall, lose their efficacy, or become demonic unless they reach out toward more than merely "experiencing one another as persons." Personalistic structures can mediate a high experience of humanness, and this is good. But freedom, joy, peace, and love are found in Jesus Christ. Not either/or—but, for me, no humanism without Christ.

And so I must speak about rebirth in the Spirit. Everything I say about newness in the body, in nature, in study and imagination, in creativity and personal identity would be meaningless if it had not been for my rebirth in the Spirit.

One of the first things Willis Elliott taught me was that what gets your attention gets you. I have never forgotten that remark. I saw so many women putting their minds to health and getting sicker and sicker, or spending their major time, effort, and thought on their work only to become disgruntled and fatigued. Many women think only of themselves, end up with no friends, alone and fearful, and wonder what happened. Others spend every free moment feeling guilty about mother (or father or someone else), and their waking hours trying to make that person happy. The result is that both lives deteriorate.

I went through this last phase and was awakened at a retreat by Dorothy Hamm of the Church of the Saviour in Washington, D.C., who said, "Don't be afraid to pick up your cross. But carry your own cross and not that of another. If you carry another's cross you keep both that person and yourself from knowing Christ."

I began to discover that as long as I kept my eye on Jesus, feasted on his actions and his word, everything ran smoothly, miracles happened, and peace abounded. As soon as I took my eye off this terrifyingly beautiful life I fumbled, the light dimmed, and I often lost my way.

How did I feast? This took many forms and has changed through the years, but gradually it has taken in all life. In the beginning I searched mainly through dialogue with other seekers, through Bible study and prayer. Gradually, I moved out to attending conferences and retreats, then growth groups where I came to know a few people at depth. Once trust in self and others and affirmation of life were established, running after Jesus took the form of obedience to living through what life offered.

CHAPTER 6

The Physical Life

A friend recently asked me what I wanted most in life. I replied, "I simply long for souls to be free."

She replied, "But it has something to do with space, a person's being free. We need to run and dance and sing and shout. We need estates in the country or playgrounds for adults. Japan has large open spaces for sports after work. Europe has large stadiums for folk dancing, running, tennis, and swimming. America has these places in small numbers, but they are so overcrowded, far apart, and expensive that they are useless for most people. And who can yell and shout surrounded so closely by others?"

Play and Exercise

Places to be physically free can serve as a secondary substitute for "stroking" and other skin contact, of which single women are sorely deprived. I discovered this recently while working in Connecticut, where my closest neighbors were fully a quarter mile away. It was a time of special pressures in my work, when it was necessary for me to be alone for long stretches of time. Now, there's no basic problem for me in being alone. I like it. But one day I noticed that my muscles were taking on the old pattern of tautness and rigidity. What to do? I walked, then I began to jog, and finally I was loping along in a half-run. I had begun to feel exhilarated and much less tired. I said something out loud. It embarrassed me at first because the sound of my voice always embarrasses me. I took myself to task. You know you shouldn't be uncomfortable with anything about yourself, said I, so talk till you get used to it.

For several days thereafter I went outdoors and walked, ran, talked, shouted. It was great. We should have running and shouting rooms in all densely populated areas! I felt a notable release of tension after each foray and a sense of joy and celebration. Each time, I returned to my work with renewed vigor and inspiration. In a mysterious manner I felt almost as though I had been loved in the process.

Dr. Elvis Stahr, President of Indiana University, recently told a group of students at Ripon College, "We tend to treat our minds as if they existed without bodies. It is surprising how little most of us know about the control and conditioning of our bodies and how it facilitates mental activity." [1] I believe it facilitates spiritual growth as well.

We *are* our bodies. We are each a unit: body-person. The body is not an object to be ignored. When we reject the body, we reject the self we are.

Many single women have desk jobs which afford them little exercise. Yet regular exercise can help one become used to the body, to feel comfortable in it. Exercising not only tones the muscles of the body and stimulates the circulation, it provides psychological and spiritual benefits as well.

Exercise should lead to exhilaration and a sense of well-being. It can be entered into alone or with groups. If you feel rusty from disuse, flabby from lack of muscle stimulation, this may be the point at which you can start on your journey to a fuller life. Strange as it may seem, this is one of the most difficult areas of discipline for persons in their middle years. This is partially true because America does not have a tradition of maintaining physical fitness as do other countries. Simple physical exercise plays a far greater role in preventing illness and deterioration than most people realize. Unfortunately, we Americans—doctors as well as other people—tend to be primarily sickness-minded. We are less interested in maintaining health, more interested in trying to cure sickness. We are undisciplined in our eating, sleeping, and exercising habits. Most of us would rather take a tranquilizer or a pep pill than really work toward good health. Most medical men who have given this subject serious consideration seem to agree that a regular program of exercise and well-balanced diet are necessary for human well-being and physical vitality. Exercise is as helpful to toning down tensions as to building muscle tone amid the tensions of contemporary society. You may not be ready to try skipping rope, bicycling, playing tennis, or doing push-ups. But most of us can start with a good brisk walk which can gradually become a jog or a run. Or we can begin with slow, rhythmic body motions similar to those used in sacred dance.

The American woman is generally noted for being well-dressed and made up and for having beautiful hair. But underneath the beautiful clothes are unnecessarily flabby muscles and, under the makeup, unnecessary lines of age and worry.

The president of Ripon College, Bernard S. Adams, said at the dedication of a new gymnasium:

> The spirit of liberal learning embraces all that is human, all that relates to the intellectual, emotional, spiritual, and physical being that we call "man." If an educational experience is to be truly "liberating," able to "free" man from the bonds of ignorance, insensitivity, and the closed mind, all parts of the human complex must find their places within a total educational program. "Physical" education then becomes a contributor not only to motor development and to general physical well-being but to the total process, the organic, interacting whole that we call liberal learning.[2]

Sex and the Body

Our pop culture says sex is the most serious reality of life. Many people give it most of their attention, worship it. The Bible stands in direct opposition to this life-style, since nothing should be given that much attention but God. Biblically, sex is characterized as natural and good because God created it so. But it is a "creature" in the sense that God gave it to woman for her use. It is relatively nonserious in comparison with personhood, to which it should be instrumental. It is nonserious in much the same way as is an arm, or an eye. If I lose an arm or an eye I'll still be a person (unless I choose not to be). It's better to have the arm or the eye, but not necessary—not *really* serious.

Sexuality, then, must derive its seriousness from something more serious, the good of man. How then do we free sexuality to be good, knowing it is potentially good? And how use this energy to serve God and our neighbor?

Pop-Freudians believe one will become frustrated without genital sexual activity. My experience, and that of many of my married friends, has been that an overabundance of sexual activity was the factor which created frustration. Making too much of genital sex also denigrates the true self and saps energy which might well be used in some more constructive way. It's true that sex with a spouse with whom one has a growing relationship is the dessert of life—the added fillip which fills one with wonder, delight, and warmth. *But persons can live without genital sex—they cannot live without community.* This is true whether a person is single or married.

A marriage may have no communion even though the couple sleeps in the same bed and copulates every night. Many single persons have mental or spiritual union with others at a deeper level than many married persons. Usually the single person is not aware that this is true because the shout of our sex-ridden culture obliterates the quiet presence of these other unions, deluding us with the notion that nongenital relationships can't be fulfilling.

Still, we must face the reality that the sex urge is a problem for most single women. We must face our tensions and needs honestly. Passion remains a problem as long as it is not directed. Left to its own disorderly devices it can play havoc with one's emotions and thus with one's whole life. On the other hand, primitive energy that it is, sex can be used creatively in many areas if controlled and directed.

Again, much of the pain and conflict which comes from deprivation of genital sex is self-inflicted. There are several aspects to this.

1. Some women simply choose to think about their lack. They allow their minds to dwell on sex by watching such film and television fare as gives them vicarious sexual thrills, feeling sorry for themselves that they have no male companion, fantasizing about how life might be, and in various other ways. When a woman lives in fantasy rather than reality, she is headed for despair. When she turns her thoughts to reality, she provides an opening for hope. This allows her to find a way to deal with her sexual frustrations without escaping into a dream world that can only destroy her.

2. Some other women decide sex is a nasty subject, too hard to deal with even under the best of circumstances. These women repress every sexual thought and feeling, or at least try to do so. They usually become moralistic and rigid. But such moralism is a dishonest effort to hide their feelings. The feelings they are hiding may be those of inadequacy, but many times they are feelings of fear: fear born of some past happening that distorted their understanding in this area of life, or fear of their own desires and emotions. Single middle-aged women, more than any other group today, become self-righteous and bitter—even cruel—in their attempt to prove their superiority to others by their abstinence from overt sexual acts. These unfortunate women, who get caught up in vindictive criticism of women who drink, smoke, or "run around," are probably more unhappy, lonely, and bitter than they would ever want to admit. It would shock them to realize that it was exactly this kind of judgment and pride which caused Jesus to say to one crowd who was condemning a "sinful" woman, "Let him who is without sin among you be the first to throw a stone at her (John 8:7)."

3. Other women act out their frustrations in various forms of overt sexuality with varying degrees of guilt and conflict. There are advantages and disadvantages in every possible relationship

Sexual Options for the Unmarried 30-and-older Woman

A. None; i.e., absolute continence; i.e., no use of the skin in giving and receiving affection

      advantages   disadvantages

B. Nongenital skin contacts with both sexes: handshaking, hugging, kissing

    1. with one's own sex

    2. with the opposite sex

C. Autoeroticism: masturbation

D. Homosexuality: covenantal

E. Homosexuality: promiscuous

F. Heterosexuality: promiscuous

G. Heterosexuality: covenantal

    1. legal marriage

    2. common-law union

    3. cohabitation

H. Ambisexuality (e.g., hippies' "group grope")

I. Spouse-sharing (with permission of marriage partner)

J. Home-raiding (adultery; without knowledge of marriage partner)

NOTE: The function of this skeletal typology is to provide an objective way of enabling discussion over the whole range of possibilities. The schema applies, of course, to all adults; but it is arranged with a particular group in mind—unmarried thirty-and-older women.

open to a single woman. It is up to each woman to choose for herself, among the options open to her, which form she prefers. I'm indebted to Dr. Elliott for the list on page 52, which he prepared for me when I first started studying the subject and trying to become free of my own bondage. I have found it helpful in counseling single women as they sort out their options.

4. Large numbers of women accept their singleness or choose it joyfully. More than half of the answers to a recent questionnaire of mine revealed that the responders are glad they are unmarried. Their reasons are various but most often included one or more of the following, listed here in order of preference: (a) more time and freedom to serve God and neighbor, (b) freedom to come and go at will, (c) freedom to pursue own desires, (d) a fulfilling job, (e) friendships beyond what one might experience in marriage. Several women indicated that they were much happier single because they were simply not meant for marriage and recognized it. Still, many of these women had "settled for" singleness rather than embraced it joyfully.

5. Finally, we must mention those women who have chosen freely the single state as a religious vocation—a special subgroup within group four. They are willing to sacrifice marriage in order to become completely available to God and to persons. Their talents and energies are devoted to and focused on the kingdom of God. They forego family in the marital sense in order to witness to a more inclusive family: the body of Christ and the oneness of mankind.

Sidney Cornelia Callahan says:

> Agreement comes from most observers that the process of personal growth can keep operating in persons who lead lives of sexual abstinence. Many such persons do not regress, but continue the process of converting erotic energy into communal love and work. Their responsiveness and cooperation with others keeps them sensitive, alert, and fulfilled. As long as the physical desire for love and unity can be sublimated

into friendship, charity, and service, as long as the physical and creative tension can be spent in creative work, the personality keeps expanding.[3]

The same author also observes that it is "in an impoverished, shallow culture with no access to art, literature, tradition, intellect, religion, athletics, work, or communal life [that]. . . sexual abstinence would be almost impossible."[4] She points out that genital sex is the only avenue of expression and fulfillment left in such cases. On the other hand, developed cultures have always had celibate persons. Persons who expend high levels of energy in other creative pursuits often find they can live happily a life free of the genital expression of sex.

Not all women should marry. Some are bodily or mentally crippled from birth. Others have been so emotionally crippled by their surroundings within the first few years of life that there seems little doubt the pressures of marriage and family would only further cripple them and the husband and children as well. Often these women can find fulfillment in creative pursuits if given the opportunity. The great unrest that dogs their tracks is often *the marriage obsession,* which the culture cruelly imposes.

Still other women have an honest desire to pursue a career rather than marry, as we have seen. These women are sometimes respected more than women who do not marry for other reasons —even envied. But unless such a woman is part of an accepting and supporting community, she does not fare much better than her sister singles. She faces the same cultural pressures to conform to the youth-and-marriage cult. Only the rare woman maintains the joy and peace of her earlier decision as these pressures create loneliness and doubt. Sooner or later she, too, may be added to the ranks of the unhappy single middle-aged woman.

Through the past few years many women have asked me how I overcame my own physical passions. I share with you here some of the devices I used to channel this energy. You may find others. (1) Confession of the struggle. It's important here to find someone you can trust or learn to trust. Trust itself can heal discontent and can discipline and channel energy. (2) Prayer and reflection in the light of the reality of the situation, and a willingness to change. (3) Exercise and deep breathing often help momentarily. Let your mind move to something else as you move about. (4) Reading a book which is not titillating. This, like exercise, is one of the least effective diversions, since it is so temporary. But anything that helps you see you will not die of the pain aids in self-control. (5) Finger painting, water-coloring, rhythmic movements, writing, singing, playing an instrument, are ways of finding yourself in the highest sense. (6) Studying the subject of sex and personhood from an academic standpoint with the purpose of learning how to use this God-given energy. (7) Learning to deal with other frustrations in your life. (8) Learning more about all forms of love, and disciplining yourself to reach out to others to help and for help. (9) Deepening relationships with a few primary persons in life is the best way I have found. (10) Attempting to use your total love-energy to serve God and your neighbor.

CHAPTER 7

Employment

Before I set my course purposefully toward the spiritual life I had, like many professional women, been living what some people would call a busy, successful life. My salary was adequate, I traveled a lot and spent many hours at theaters, dinner parties, concerts, ball games, and so on. Most people seemed to think I was satisfied, if they thought about it at all. But inside me was a vague emptiness, a hollowness, a shell of intellectualism which kept me from having close relationships.

It was equally true that even though I held jobs of responsibility —assistant to a publisher, assistant to the president of a medium-sized corporation—I was paid, in each case, less than half the amount a man would have been paid in the same position. Because men did not accept me, or any woman, as simply another person working alongside them, I was either "very special" and felt embarrassed or was ignored almost completely and could not, therefore, do an adequate job. I experienced many of the slights, embarrassments, and injustices mentioned in the July 1968 *Saturday Evening Post* article "Is There Room at the Top?"—a fair appraisal of the present condition, which is, incidentally, somewhat superior to that of a decade earlier. This article quotes one woman as saying that although her title sounds great, she is still "just a glorified secretary." That's what great numbers of women with tremendous potential turn out to be.

As I discovered, there are three factors especially debilitating to the personality. The first has been described by Herbert Marcuse as "work that amounts to exhausting, stupefying, inhuman slavery. Being pressed to maximum efficiency irrespective of personhood." [1] In a like vein, Professor Eric Fromm said recently on TV,

"Maximum efficiency carries with it minimum humanity." The work system is treating the human being like a machine or a part —a thing. A friend from Europe said to me, "Here in America we are treated like dogs. 'Can you do this? Can you do that? Jump, sit, speak.'"

The problem is complicated by the fact that the majority of persons today are bored by their jobs. Boredom breeds loss of efficiency (including pettiness, bickering, and gossip). Loss of efficiency creates a tendency in the system to push for greater efficiency; the worker feels this push, becomes anxious and less efficient—and round and round we go.

In our culture a woman must be a very exceptional person in order to excel in the working world where she is merely a functional unit. Particularly as an executive or a professional, she is "in" just as long as she can perform better, follow the right leads, cultivate the right people. Her inner life shrinks in such an atmosphere. Competition is often so strong that she becomes anxious about her adequacy and worried about failure. This worry is exaggerated in the middle years, for she knows that now not only are her sex and singleness against her but also her age.

I am told that some of the women employees in a church agency now and then joke about the ability of sexy girls to turn on the ministers in the organization (this situation being not unlike that of various secular jobs in which I have worked). This may be amusing, but it is also sad—when related to the middle-aged church worker who devotes her life to the church.

The sexy young girl in any organization is more or less a decoration; the middle-aged woman does most of the work. The higher the middle-aged single woman rises in such a set-up, the more difficult her life becomes. She is expected to be creative, to work harder than her male colleagues, to "manage" other women for whom she is responsible, while all the time she is treated as an inferior person by her boss and by her male co-workers. Because she is treated badly, she finds it hard to deal constructively with people and situations.

Young girls will be sweet with the men but will be flip and antagonistic toward older women. If any personality conflict arises, the male boss will usually side with the young girl. Or worse yet, he will not even discuss the matter with the older woman, but simply assume that she is in the wrong because she is middle-aged and therefore hard to get along with or because she is envious of the young girl. The middle-aged single woman becomes so burdened with unjust prejudices and unreasonable expectations that very often she gives in to one of many introversive escapes.

The second factor debilitating to the personality is the necessity of competing in a man's world as a male rather than being allowed to work alongside the man as a human being, making full use of the particular gifts each woman brings to her situation. The frustration which results often causes the woman to react aggressively. When she feels discriminated against, her manner becomes unattractive: some women become domineering and hard, while others tend to be emotional.

A friend of mine is in the hospital chaplaincy. Certainly dealing with the sick is a woman's business. Yet she is allowed only inferior status and is paid less than her talents warrant. Willis Elliott said to her recently, "It's cruel for you to have to compete in your profession with the male image of the chaplaincy when the female gifts are more appropriate for the chaplaincy than the male, so you have a double occasion for rage against the situation. Women more naturally understand human relations and are naturally better chaplains than men. And you not only have to face this double injustice but also, and more perilously, the negative feelings within yourself that these cause."

Claire Randall, Director of National Program Development for Church Women United, said to me recently, "The problem is that we are not working as women but as emasculated men. The patterns as to what you do and how you do it, whether in a business office, in a law office, or in the church, have all been set by men. This keeps women from being who they really are when they are forced to make this kind of adjustment, and so they cannot function to their best capacity. If we women are to get into the decision-making, we must do it without aping what has been."

Cynthia Wedel, Associate General Secretary for Christian Unity for the National Council of Churches, says in *Sex, Family and Society in Theological Focus:*

> If either a man or a woman in a work situation looks upon the other only as a sexual object there are many possibilities of trouble. Yet if sexuality can be accepted freely and naturally, women can bring to business many valuable qualities. The world of work will be enriched by the presence of women if they can be feminine in the best sense of the word, that is, strong, gentle, concerned with individuals, sympathetic, patient. In the present transitional period this is sometimes difficult because practices and standards in the world of work are still masculine, and often require a woman to be unfeminine if she is to conform.[2]

Third, there is a deep-seated sex prejudice which causes men to be threatened by the existence of women in "a man's world," and which causes them to treat women in negative ways. Women soon learn to prefer the blatant insults and rejections to the subtle ones, for the latter are almost impossible to deal with constructively.

Almost all single women have to work. Many support not only themselves but also parents and/or other members of the family. Increasingly, single women are supporting children here and abroad who have been left homeless from one of the many forms of tragedy and devastation stalking the globe. Still, women are looked upon as something less than their male counterparts and are paid accordingly.

The struggle to be real and adequate under unnatural conditions forces a woman to hide her feelings. The pressures of modern society may make her feel hostile; but having no outlet for these destructive feelings she begins to destroy herself in many ways. The potential within for fulfillment and service is destroyed at its roots.

Further, there are often small occurrences which ominously sap at a woman's inner self-respect. They are being aired below because this type of prejudiced behavior not only exists but is common. Prejudice against the woman really works against the man in lack of efficiency and interest on the part of women in the work they are trying to do; an encrustation and narrowing of the man's own personality and spontaneity; fatigue brought on by toleration of a situation with which he is not at home; a certain amount of guilt, whether he is aware of this or not, engendered by abuse of a person.

Vignettes follow:

A professor of a theological seminary asks me if we could have lunch some noon so he could hear about my work. It is the first time in eight years that a man has volunteered in such a manner to learn what I was doing. The day arrives. I am on time for the meeting. He calls to say he has someone else with him and cannot have lunch with me. A few minutes later we all happen to leave the building at the same time—the third person is a man. Countless women have told me similar stories.

. . .

I approach a clerk to ask a question or get directions in a library, a drugstore, a bank—anywhere. A man approaches and, although I arrived first, the man's wishes or questions are satisfied before mine.

. . .

I arrive at the office of a prominent New York City pastor for an appointment of several weeks' standing and am announced, on time. A man walks in. The man tells the girl at the desk he would like to see the pastor. The pastor walks out, glances at me, ushers the man into his office.

. . .

A middle-aged single woman who holds a job of considerable responsibility is discussing some business matters with a male colleague who has come to her office. A second man walks in, invites the man to have lunch with him, and completely ignores the woman.

. . .

Recently a talented friend of mine was telling a couple she hadn't seen since college days how much work she did nights and weekends and how she hoped this would soon change. The husband answered, "But what would you have to do if you didn't bring work home?"

. . .

An interesting paradox occurs at this point. Many women discriminate against other women even more than men discriminate against them.

There are some women who flatly refuse to work for another woman. It is true that most women bosses expect more of women than men do—a woman executive has to accomplish more to be accepted. A male boss is often easier to get along with and expects less because—unconsciously perhaps—he considers women to be inferior. There is no doubt that some women bosses are, for reasons already made clear, difficult persons. But it is important for women to realize that if they treated women bosses as well and as graciously as they treat men bosses, women bosses would be easier to live with.

The businesswoman over fifty-five may see a woman co-worker between thirty and fifty-five as a threat, and become unpleasant as a result. The older woman can compete with the girl under thirty because sex is no longer too important in her life and because her business experience helps her to know more than the young girl. The older woman cannot fight the men, so she takes out her frustrations on women peers who are closer to her age. Self-awareness may enable her to rid herself of this destructive attitude.

Women could do a great deal to help one another in the working world. If they tried, they would surely find work conditions and relationships improving.

There are numberless ways in which the sex prejudice appears outside offices. Restauranteurs and taxi drivers almost invariably give first service and best service to men. At posh restaurants men or couples are given choice seats whether or not the woman has phoned ahead for reservations.

It's good to observe the male-female imbalance beginning to equalize. Mutuality implies give and take, and should do away with the imposition of authority, whether of master over slave, man over woman, or white over black. Unless single women come into the decision-making process of life, they remain marginal, downtrodden, and weak. Every weak link in the chain of society makes the society itself weaker.

God has made us male or female. One of the basic marks of a person's maturity is the extent to which he or she can accept, appreciate, develop, and express the talents with which he or she has been endowed. Our acceptance of one another with trust, gratitude, and joy will foster maturity and the use of talents.

CHAPTER 8

Asking the Right Questions

It is important for you, the single woman, to answer thought-provoking questions about your real values and state in life. It is just as important for you to *ask* questions.

But *are you asking the right questions?* You may be asking the wrong questions about matters which affect you deeply. If the questions are wrong, the answers will also be wrong.

Are you asking: "Why doesn't anyone love me?" Change the question around and ask, "Do I truly love anyone? Do I love anyone in an unselfish, nonjudgmental manner?" If your answer is no, then you have the answer to your first question. There may be nothing you can do about getting someone to love you until you do something about loving someone else.

Are you asking: "What would I be interested in doing?" Ask instead, "What needs to be done that I can do? Where can I be of use; where are my talents and skills needed?"

It's true that millions of women do social work and volunteer work of all kinds, and society has not evaluated what women are doing and what they might do more than they are doing. This general ignorance makes it harder for you to find a place where you can use your potential. Still, giving the question a new twist will be helpful.

Are you asking: "Why don't I have any fun? Why is life so dull?" If you've asked this for some time and have found no viable answer, try giving the question a new twist. Ask instead, "Just how interested am I in life? How can I become more interested?" The fact that you ask the question in itself will be a help, since a person must first become aware of a problem before she begins to find an answer. It is by our own choice that we have interest in a thing or a feeling or an attitude.

If the world around you is gray, events dull, and life itself meaningless, it's because you have sifted out of your life the very things which would make it meaningful and interesting. It's true that you may have done this without being aware of it. Nevertheless, through the choices you have made, you have created what you now possess, and a gap exists between your desire for fun and meaning and the actuality of dullness and boredom. This gap desperately needs to be closed if your life is to be worthwhile to yourself or to others. You need to enter purposefully into the development of some interest beyond yourself. You actually need a passionate dedication to and interest in *some cause* which you can serve. You need something to draw you away from yourself and to absorb the interest you place in yourself. If you do not achieve this you will die spiritually, and slowly other functions will die also. You will become more and more bored and dull until you die to creative sensation, to life itself.

The fruition of interest, however, closes the gap. This is one of the most important clues to wholeness and to joy.

As I watched a political convention in 1968 I was struck with the energy and zeal the politicians exuded. Many presidents, great inventors, and saints seem to have required little sleep— some only three or four hours a night. Undoubtedly much such stamina stems from passionate interest in something beyond oneself and from a greater use of one's potential and a greater participation in life than most of us ever manage.

Do not blame others for the dullness of your life. At this very moment there are great amounts of "forgotten" or rejected material in your unconscious which can be helpful to you in learning to live a dynamic, interesting life. It needs your willingness to ask the right questions, to begin to develop what you already possess in the rich and fertile field of the unconscious, and to bear the pain of learning to live life anew.

To allow your imagination to flower and grow, ask yourself

unusual questions. "What would it feel like to be a spring?" "What does the color red *feel* like?" "What kind of shapes can I *see* in clouds?" "What is nice to *touch?*" "What is different about early morning sounds—light—smells?" Make up a few of your own.

Can we recapture some of the freshness and energy of the child by using some ingenuity in our questioning? The child surprises us by the quality of his questioning, by his awe and wonder before life. But while we are attempting to recreate our lost childlike qualities of wonder and curiosity, let us not, like the child, allow the first answer or the easiest answer to suffice. The child's wonder tends to be fleeting—sometimes he does not really care about an answer, does not even wait for one. A child does not see the problems involved in the questions he asks. His interest is momentary and not deep. His dedication to discover the true answer is nil. Thus, using a combination of freshness and energy with sustained interest, you might like to ask yourself some of the following questions:

Questions on Personhood

1. How do I see myself right now? How would I like to see myself?

2. What am I looking forward to in the next twenty-four hours?

3. Who or what would I like to avoid during the next twenty-four hours?

4. How did I spend my past weekend? What does this tell me about my values? About my desires?

5. When did I, during the past week, either act out, or fail to act out when I wanted to, the way I was feeling? What values were involved? Were they my own values? If they were not, whose were they?

6. Was I envious during the last week? About what or whom? What does this tell me?

7. Was I angry during the last twenty-four hours? Why? At whom? What does this tell me about myself?

8. Do I live up to values and standards which are not my own? If so, what ones? How can I learn to live up to my own values?

9. When, in the past twenty-four hours, did I choose to act as a free, responsible person, speaking up for what I believe? If I did not speak up, why not?

10. For what event in the past am I most grateful?

11. At what or whom in my past am I still angry? What can I do about it?

12. When was I most afraid? Recall the incident fully.

13. When did I feel most guilty? About whom or what? Why?

14. When did I feel most rejected? Who rejected me?

15. Am I bound to one event in my past? One person?

16. How do I react at the theater? Do I *think* or *feel?*

17. What are the heights I have known? What heights would I like to know?

18. What are the depths I have known? What depths would I like to know?

CHAPTER 9
Participation

We need to look into the future and begin to create new structures which will alleviate the ills of the present. We need to do some idol-smashing and some rugged pioneering. We desperately need to demythologize, deromanticize, desentimentalize marriage, the family, sex. We have made these our sacred cows, along with youth and success; now the sacred cows are milking *us* dry!

Besides the suggestions already given, there are a variety of *practical ways* in which women can be encouraged and helped to become greater participants in our culture, using their massive potential for good in the service of a better society. These suggestions by no means exhaust the possibilities. They are presented in the hope that they will serve as openers to something more.

Education

As early as 1933 Carl Jung said:

> Are there perhaps colleges for forty-year-olds which prepare them for their coming life and its demands? . . . Our religions were always such schools in the past, but how many people regard them as such today? How many of us older persons have really been brought up in such a school and prepared for the second half of life, for old age, death, and eternity?[1]

And John W. Gardner, Chairman of the Urban Coalition, formerly Secretary of Health, Education, and Welfare for the

Federal Government, has said that we ought to have mid-career clinics for people over thirty-five or so who want to take a look at what they are accomplishing and where they are headed in life.

Many adult women today have in common an urgent need for further education, notwithstanding differences in aptitude, interest, experience, or background. The available educational opportunities fall far short of this need, and bridging the gap is a critical necessity if womanpower is to be activated.

Technological change is fast creating new jobs which require education and training, while at the same time old jobs are being erased from our culture. Often basic learning must come before any technical training. In the *Report of the Committee on Education of the President's Commission on the Status of Women* for October 1963, we read: "Eight million adults over the age of 18 are considered functionally illiterate. They have had less than 5 years of formal schooling and cannot fill out a simple job application form. Three and seven-tenths million of them are women. Millions more have failed to finish high school." [2]

To help not only the person with no education but the educated woman who needs additional training to bring her abreast of the times, we need *imagination and experimentation in adult education*. The opportunities for mature women to continue their education should be greatly expanded and adapted to their needs.

The above-mentioned report made six recommendations which all women should be aware of and promote. Colleges, universities, and vocational, technical, and professional schools should work toward:

1. The acceptance and encouragement of part-time study through such measures as grants of financial aid and increased flexibility in working out individual schedules.

2. Reexamination of policies on admission, academic prerequisites, transfer of credits, and graduation requirements (including such nonacademic requirements as residence and physical education).

3. Wider use of proficiency testing and other means to give

credit for knowledge and experience acquired outside regular academic channels.

4. The establishment of bridging courses to rebuild habits of study, introduce new techniques, and provide the background and confidence for contemporary study and work.

5. The development of educational guidance services to help the mature woman deal with the problems and opportunities of resumed study and a possible second career.

6. The creation of special programs to prepare mature women to work in fields where their aptitudes and urgent social needs coincide, such as in teaching and nursing.[3]

The last recommendation is particularly important since, at our point in history, it is specifically womanpower our world needs.

We are only now, in this generation, beginning to come into a genuine appreciation of mutuality between the sexes. We are painfully coming to the awareness that fulfilling human relationships between men and women, whether in family or at work, can never be reached when there is domination of one sex over the other. Man and woman were created equal persons. Each person, whether male or female, has a destiny to fulfill, a work to do, a gift to use in building up the society of man and living creatively. Our society will never be truly human, nor will it come to full stature, until we learn to live in such a way that man and woman are equal sharers in society as they are in humanity— that they bear equal responsibility and allow each other equal freedom. The goals of full womanhood and full manhood—full personhood—are unattainable when the sexes are separated geographically, psychologically, or spiritually.

Life-Style

If we are to develop as a nation and as a people we must *open all areas of life to every human being.* We need imaginative new education which will bridge gaps in our nation and world. As we have seen, a great deal of the so-called "sickness" among middle-aged women is due to boredom which arises when they do not or are not allowed to use their true potential; when they have no purpose in life and feel they are not needed. There are innumerable ways the society and church can encourage and enable women to feel and live differently, just as the ideas which women can bring forth and nourish are inexhaustible.

By and large the single woman has not picked up her option to *choose her own life-style*. Feeling a failure because she is not married, she drifts or charges through life (depending upon her proclivities), often wishing she were something she is not or doing something she is not doing. As a member of a so-called democratic society she is supposed to be free to choose. Of course her freedom creates an obligation to assume corresponding responsibility. If she does not assume this responsibility or accept her freedom she becomes a slave to the establishment which may not be *for* her interests, but *against* them.

We need women who will work with more enthusiasm both at their jobs and in their places of residence to bring about a better world for all of us. It is a well-known fact that one reason women as a group do not advance faster in politics and business, for example, is that they do not try hard enough. The average woman does not prefer to work, whether she is single or married. More often than not women work for economic reasons and nothing more. Without enthusiasm for their work there is no vision. Men notice this and soon come to feel that women have no place outside the home.

Women must *become vocal* about the changes they want made and the injustices they see and feel. We need women who will not be afraid to involve themselves in matters which do not affect them personally but which will be of benefit to the larger society.

If we women want others to develop confidence in our ability to contribute to our society, we must do something to bring this about. We must be willing to think about our situation with others, discuss it—not complain and gripe. In a cooperative spirit we must work toward changes in our own attitudes, so that the attitudes of others will be changed toward us. Our future will be as good as the effort we put into making it good. The climate is right for change.

Another attitude women must change is their tendency to pseudomodesty: a deprecation of their accomplishments and potential. In both business and politics the opposite set of attitudes is required. A woman must have confidence in herself and in her charisma—a confidence which says, "I feel this is right to do and I am going to do it." This will undoubtedly mean she must be prepared for criticisms and for expanding her interests and knowledge.

Involvement in Humanity

Above all, women need to involve themselves in humanity. Walk down to your city's Emergency Child Welfare Service (ECW), which is open all night every night and around the clock on weekends, to see what is going on there. Observe the despair of deprived mothers and deprived and starved children. Take some other women with you. You'll discover a whole new world, as well as something you can do if you put your minds to work.

Try sitting in a session of night court, or visit an old people's home, an orphanage, a coffeeshop which caters to disenchanted youth. Don't just read your newspaper or watch TV—go feel and smell these places. If you have not crushed your womanhood completely you will be compelled to do something. And anything at all is a start toward both personal growth and the alleviation of distortion in the social situation.

Once your heart has been opened to some specific area of need, you must *educate* yourself to the dimensions of the problem. You can do this by reading, by listening to what responsible news analysts and civic leaders have to say about the situation. You may want to join or lend support to community efforts or citizens' organizations that are making strides toward licking the problem. Or you may want to start a group yourself.

Society and the church can aid a woman to renew and re-
vitalize her *imagination*. Seldom is it dead; it only smolders
among the dead ashes of inactivity. If the fire does at last go out,
she dies. She then becomes a ward of the state in some old people's home or asylum or she literally dies at too early an age,
possibly by her own hand.

Let's allow our imagination to rove. There are millions of
children who need homes—children deserted on streets and in
hospitals and in county homes for unwanted children. Pearl S.
Buck has written about some of them:

> I am setting down these thoughts after a visit to a great
> city hospital. One part of it houses children, although they are
> not physically ill. They were born there in the hospital and
> were never taken away because no one wants them. I walked
> between the cribs. The children lie in strange silence, listen-
> ing. To what? I listened too. I heard a mechanical heart, a
> machine in the wall. Its beat simulates the beat of a mother's
> heart before her child is born. The sound keeps the children
> quiet. They remain unborn.[4]

In an article entitled "Miracle on 12th Street," Jack Shepherd
gives the following statistics on the mentally ill child.

> There are more than 4.5 million emotionally disturbed
> and mentally ill children. The National Institute of Mental
> Health counts half a million psychotic or borderline young-
> sters. . . .
>
> In Los Angeles County schools, 33.2 percent of the chil-
> dren need treatment. But there are no facilities for them.
>
> The Washington, D.C. school system spots about 6,000 dis-
> turbed kids each year. Few get help. . . .
>
> Neglect is costly. The price of mental illness runs to $3
> billion a year.[5]

Instead of allowing this inhuman condition to exist at such high cost to us both financially and in human potential, why not set up training programs for single women who can learn to care for and deal with these children? Basically, the children need a home, love, and attention, while women need to give love which is being extinguished in the center of their ashheap of boredom. Many women could, in this way, fulfill their destiny to be mothers.

Criteria could be set up in which women who were not qualified would drop out during some stage of the new education (just as we have dropouts in all areas of learning).

After a period of training, which would need to be at odd hours for women who work, women themselves would find ways in which to use their newfound talent and interest. (1) You might volunteer spare hours in institutions such as hospitals, homes for unwed mothers, homes for unwanted children, social agencies, and so forth. (2) You might become helpful in finding a more humane way to deal with the fast-growing problems of the unwed mother and the unwanted child. (3) You could set up day-care centers for working mothers who must earn a living for their children. (4) Homes might be established where you and several other women could make a home for children, living like any mother whose husband is gone from the home. There could be monthly supervision and further help for the women involved. The supervisor and women could learn from one another in a continuing dialogue—the supervisor seeking further growth in understanding and skills. It would be better if the supervisors could be men who would spend time with the children as well.

Similar plans could be worked out for the elderly and the handicapped. Or possibly you are not interested in working with people so much as alleviating injustices and bridging other gaps in our society. You may be more concerned with conserving precious natural resources, ensuring justice in the police department, beautifying your city, disposing of air pollution, violence on TV, and so forth. You need not feel you can do nothing! Find another woman (or three or four if you can) and together get some facts concerning the situation which troubles you. Find out who it is in your locality who has responsibility for your area of concern. Go to the persons and talk with them. You can and will find a way to help if you are truly interested in making an imprint on the world before you leave it. And there are innumerable stories of women who have made not an imprint but an impact on their communities.

Community

Most single women over thirty live in a subculture as tough as that of poverty: a culture where there is a *poverty of relationships*. It is a way of life massively guarded against the hurts of the world. It produces a sad ambivalence: the singler wants "fellowship," but no change in her way of life. Yet her need for deep relationships is often acute.

Dialogue is central to the redemptive community. It is the tool by means of which members of differing viewpoints can take one another seriously for the sake of their common tasks as well as for personal growth and global rejuvenation. It is one way to form deep relationships. Thus, each woman in a discussion group or community must bring to the others not only her feelings and fears but her best thinking and hopes as well. Honesty in dialogue is costly, for it calls for a contrite heart and a willingness to be changed. These will move the single woman toward servant-action—feeding the poor, clothing the naked, giving drink to the thirsty. The one thing necessary is that the center of community not be person-worship.

The great error will come if, once again, the institutions of the world are remade and not the hearts of men and women. Yet the transformation of just one person always produces social repercussions. A commitment or a reappraisal which changes one person at depth spreads, and society itself becomes changed.

In each small center of dynamic change a new beauty and a new order emerge. As a person moves out of herself, an extraordinary awareness begins to develop. She feels not only unique but part of an exciting and larger whole. She finds her role.

To live the true single life takes *great inner strength and deep conviction.* Without a caring community around her, how can a woman face reality and disperse the hidden inner poisons to realize something larger than herself?

I have asked dozens of single women the question: "If you had what you really longed for deep within, what would that be?" Most of the answers ran in this vein: "To be relieved of this feeling of hopelessness, this awful deadness. Once again to be able to *feel* something." "To belong to someone or something. I feel so cut off." "Fellowship." "Someone, anyone, to care what happens to me."

Since society provides her no niche—no "family" where members are involved in intimate, face-to-face association—the single woman, especially in large cities, will need to take the initiative in finding or creating such a group.

To be redemptive, such groups or "communities" will often need to be highly flexible. A singler might have only one such group, or she could have more. These communities might be formed where she lives, works, studies, or takes her leisure. Some communities might have a stationary base such as an apartment, a house, a church. Others could emerge out of an interest or an activity such as a bookstore (the Grail is successful in this regard), an eating establishment, volunteer service. Some groups might own no buildings, travel light, and leave when the work is done (as some Roman Catholic nuns now do). The variations on this theme are endless.

There is a growing body of persons who recognize that a human being needs others with whom to hammer out in actual practice what it means to love and allow oneself to be loved, to pool efforts toward a goal which will have meaning. Most of these experimental communities have a purpose for coming together beyond the fellowship and companionship the community provides. A sampling is listed below.

1. Kirkridge,[6] though older than most, is an example of the retreat and conference type of community. It describes itself as "a Christian group under a discipline, a retreat-and-study center on the Appalachian ridge, a movement for power within the church." The administrators and employees of this center live in community the year round.

2. Emmaus House [7] in New York City is "a house of reconciliation attempting to bring together men and women in a divided world. . . . Christians of different confessions [and races] in an atmosphere of prayer, friendship, and common service . . . [witness] to the oneness in Christ. . . . Our openness is to something *new* happening in dialogue, in service to the world, in commonly celebrating the living presence of Christ in the world."

3. Ann Ryan of San Antonio, Texas has recently published "New Communities of Men and Women," in which she has gathered information concerning Roman Catholic nuns who are experimenting in various forms of community life outside the monastic institution. She says:

> "Forming a community" does not necessarily mean getting a house together, choosing a name, setting up rules. . . . A new group can be started whenever two persons feel a common bond. Several groups of two or more may begin in the same city, each with their own form of life, but by frequent contact with these other equally dedicated persons, they will have the support and interest of a large community.[8]

Miss Ryan has formed what she calls an "information center" for all new communities and hopes that groups of Protestant women and groups of men will join in the spirit of community with the Catholic Women and that each will support and encourage the others. Protestant women can glean some valuable information from these pages if they are interested in experimenting with viable forms of community living themselves.

4. The Ecumenical Institute of Chicago [9] has a major concern for "a reconstruction of life-attitudes, a reeducation of the imagination for self-images relevant to the actual world . . . so that he [the person] can appropriate a sense of significance in involving himself in the drama of civilization." Families and singles share the life of the community: its joys, sorrows, work, recreation, and worship. The key to community renewal, as they see it, is "educating the ghetto resident out of the notion of himself as a victim and seeing the possibilities he has of controlling his own destiny." [10] This experiment in community living has been flourishing for several years.

5. Reba Place Fellowship, Evanston, Illinois [11] purposes to be a group of people who are living out their lives in "obedience to the Christian Gospel." It is a community composed of families and single persons who have purchased and/or rent property in a one-block area. The people have committed themselves to "support one another in the decisions we are facing," and to "take counsel together in the spirit of a common search for God's will."

6. Apple Farm, Three Rivers, Michigan "came into being as a focal point for a number of women who already had been drawn together by common interests and values." [12] There are no specific rules or formal conditions of membership, but "each woman has accepted the obligation to speak her feelings and hear the truth of another's, be they 'good' or 'bad,' and to carry responsibility for them. In short, the Apple Farm exists to nourish in all its members the inner meaning of true community." [13]

7. There is a growing interest in communities for widows. (a) Martha Harre in Washington, D.C. felt she wanted to create a place for widows to live for a season in which they would have A Place. She puts it this way:

> A place to weep,
> A place to grieve,
> A place to put down one's full weight;
> A place where one dares to look at her total life
> within the reality of her loss;

A place to look at the dreams that will never come
true, the tender memories and joys that have been;
  A place to feel the pangs and stabs of guilt,
    regret, and bitterness, and the fear
      of the days that lie ahead;
A place where one learns to walk toward life again;
  A place where one learns to walk alone
    without being lonely;
A place where one begins to sense anew the beauty
  and rhythm of her own created being,
    her gifts, her mission.[14]

(b) THEO, Inc.[15] in Pittsburgh is a venture for the widowed woman on a wider scale, being more institutionally oriented. Begun by Mrs. Bea Decker as "an organization to aid and assist those in a widowed state and their families, intellectually, morally, spiritually, and socially; [it] also provides information on widowhood, helps solve common problems, and assists families in adjusting for the future."

8. Synanon, with houses on both the east and west coast; Daytop Village, Staten Island, New York; East Ridge, Callicoon, New York, and many other communities are aiding not only drug addicts and alcoholics but "normal" citizens as well to kick tenacious habits and addictions of attitude and feeling which keep them from living life fully here and now.

9. There are many experiments in what is coming to be called "the larger Christian family." The Kennedy family has been an excellent model of the power and cohesiveness which is generated when persons support and help one another. But groups do not need to be blood relatives to experiment with family-style living arrangements. I know of a number of instances where two or more families decided to pool money, efforts, and living space. Some of these groups have included single persons, others have not. Most of them have included children. None that I am aware of, however, have included the elderly.

Stephen Rose, former editor of *Renewal* magazine, makes this suggestion: "Move several families into a specific area, perhaps using a common apartment as a center." [16] (I would hope these might include singles. They might even start with singles.) Mr. Rose further suggests that each community have as its focus some constructive effort to influence change in some vital area of life. There might be more than one focus, or the focus might change from time to time. Financing can be worked out in a variety of ways.

Volunteering

Church Women United [17] can provide information on how to begin a dialogue group and how to enroll teams of women to become actively responsible agents of reconciliation. *On Our Way Together* says: "Employed women [can] plan a group of Search Parties . . . in which all kinds of businesswomen come together with others for a couple of hours over an early supper" [18] or breakfast, or on a weekend. These women might study and act on any of the following areas of concern, or some other which is not listed here.

1. The One Per Cent Program for Development promotes understanding of the problems of international economics, international resentments (particularly in reference to the United States), and the challenge of assisting the development of emerging nations.

2. The Metropolis is a new form of society today. "We must find ways in which the power of love and hope can face down the power of bitterness and despair in 'action with' people. So, 'Wake up . . . speak up . . . move on' into action." [19]

3. The Peace Alert Team is a group of women willing to give time and thought to matters of justice and peace.

4. The Adult Literacy Program.

5. Monitoring Mass Media. This program helps women learn to recognize the impact of media of today's society; offers church

women an opportunity to express opinions in a concerted way; and gives suggestions for action women can take to encourage radio, TV, and the press to be more responsible in its content.

6. Dialogues of Discovery attempt to bridge the gaps in cultural or ethnic or age or economic areas.

7. The Civic Responsibility or Legislative Affairs Committee aids persons in knowing what legislation has been passed and to see that it is enforced, assists in developing public opinion so that people can make their own choices responsibly, and in other ways helps the woman to become better acquainted with the government of our nation, which both reflects and shapes our society.

8. Planning for and understanding ecumenical development and ecumenical living. This involves a growing understanding of the traditions of others.

9. A Well is a group of women who voluntarily make a covenant with each other to:

Set aside a period of time to meet regularly over a period of weeks.

Learn to listen to what others are saying "for real."

Keep in confidence individual problems.

Study passages of scripture together, allowing each person to share in their interpretation.

Seek to see God in the midst of everyday life and celebrate in the group's own way through worship.

Discuss requirements for Christian obedience in our world.[20]

A Well may be self-starting, as a businesswoman opens her apartment for a breakfast or a supper fellowship; a woman calls on others in her hotel, her apartment house, her block, or in the laundromat. It may arise in some more neutral fashion which cuts across racial or religious lines.

For those of you who are not yet ready to commit yourself to a group of people for any reason, there is still something you can do to become a change agent and to learn to live more fully yourself.

Dozens of already existing governmental organizations need womanpower. Some of these are the Job Corps, Neighborhood Youth Corps, Work-Study Program, Adult Basic Education Program, Volunteers in Service to America (VISTA), Community Action Program, Head Start, Upward Bound, Migrant Worker Assistance, Health Service Centers.

Volunteer help is needed in hospitals, children's homes, Golden Age clubs, and organizations such as the First Aid Squad, American Red Cross, American Cancer Society, and many others.

If you desire something to which you can give a bit more personally, FISH might be the organization. This is a "caring in action" program in which volunteers engage in such activities, on an emergency basis, as: babysitting, providing a meal, transportation, or companionship for the sick or elderly, performing housework and home repairs for the sick, reading to someone with a vision problem, and many other personal services.

The Shared Life

Every human being is meant to share her life. A person cannot be fulfilled or find meaning alone. We are all dependent on one another not only for meaning in life but for our own identity. Our need for one another is built into our nature—an essential ingredient to well-being. As God says, "It is not good that man [woman] should be alone (Gen. 2:18) " or, as Charles Davis puts it: "Now primary groups are recognized as fundamental in forming the social personality and ideals of the individual. . . . Without primary groups Christianity cannot strike deep roots." [21]

It was at seminary that my ideas about community living came into focus, teaching me that communities (primary groups, fellowships, *koinonia*) can be either healthy or unhealthy. My need for fellowship and community seemed to grow by my being thrust into dormitory life with thirty girls, all much younger than myself. But it early became quite clear that these young women did not want a mother hanging around. I made a vow to myself then and there that I would not allow myself to become "mother to the brood."

Not until the second year was well along did some of the younger girls begin to let the bars down and become friendly. Four of us in particular were drawn together in a close-knit and compatible union of interest in a particular class. We met every chance we could find to discuss the class, ourselves, other students, and everybody's reactions and feelings about almost everything. Unfortunately, each of us was at a different stage of development, and each was bent on pursuing her own personal problem and her own personal interest in the subjects we were discussing.

How the heart deceives the mind! Consciously I had made a strong effort not to let the group think of me as big sister or mother or counselor, but the pull of my heart had led me unwittingly to assume these roles. I was consumed in the total group process and the group need. My personality was not stable enough at the time, nor my knowledge sufficient, to absorb and deal with the hostilities, conflicts, and fears of the others. Eventually, abandonment of the group allegiance was the only recourse I had to save what individuality I had attained. Each member of the group was devouring the others, and the group was devouring me.

Each of us in our need for acceptance and community had rushed to depths of relationship which the group could not support. We spoke a great deal about involvement and dialogue (which became gossip at many points) and commitment (of which we had none, not even to one another). We made confessions to one another and to the group. We talked about the love of Jesus without acting in love ourselves. Our psychological and spiritual needs and demands taxed the bonds of our communality because the need for personal love—the intimate, direct relation of two persons—could not be satisfied within the group.

We became comfortable with one another—a "snob group." There were three other girls who wanted "in," and on occasion we "allowed" their participation. But because we were unable to open out to others in acceptance and love, we destroyed ourselves as a community.

Of the seven women involved, four were receiving counseling from the professor whose class we all attended. I still wonder if something of a deepening relationship might have been salvaged if we could have talked as a group with this professor as arbitrator. At least two of us suggested this, but the meeting never materialized. It seems to me that every seminary needs a spiritual adviser for such instances. A crisis is an opportunity for growth and healing. Without a cure the destructive patterns occur over and over again until healing does come or a person gives up trying.

At any rate, each of us confused three aspects which are necessary for a mature person and for formation of viable communities: (1) the person's own unique self; (2) her intimate person-to-person relationships; (3) her caring for the group as a whole. This combined confusion led to great frustrations and an inadequate understanding of what was going on. The frustrations built up into anger against ourselves, against one another, and against the group as a whole.

Each of us was attempting to solve her own problems of identity through the group process. This did little for our individual maturation, but much to destroy the group's cohesiveness. If we had had guidance from a more objective person, one not so involved, if we had had a clear commitment to one another, or if we had had more understanding of the need for true honesty and openness, we might have become a primary group. But such was not the case. Each of us had needs which were too deep and too demanding for the group to handle. Fellowship, which had been the original aim, was trampled underfoot.

Also, our goals were not solid enough to build a firm foundation. We were running to one another like little children, clinging to one another. More often than not what we shared with one another was no more important than a bit of gossip. The group itself had no identity. We had no way of testing our group experience against that of other groups and therefore were unable to test the reality of what we were doing and/or accomplishing as a group. Our own hostility and needs actually escaped us through self-deception because, in reality, we had no community.

One Monday morning after class we all congregated to share a cup of tea and insights on the day's lectures, as was our habit. For several weeks my sleep and studies had been suffering because I had been spending many hours listening to the problems of these young women, taking on unconsciously that maternal role I had decided against. This particular morning I was exhilarated from the lecture, weary from lack of sleep. My head was resting on the back of a chair. I felt blissfully content. It seemed to me, for the moment, I had seldom been so happy. A woman over forty-five who two years ago felt life was over was now surrounded by young, vibrant girls; engaged in satisfying conversation; mellowed by good fellowship and growing love—such were my misinformed thoughts. Into my semisomnambulent state, bordering on euphoria, came the voice of my favorite "daughter." It was harsher than usual, and it was accusing me of something. I struggled to awaken myself. I do not recall the words she spoke, I recall only the expression of anger and hostility, of complete alienation, on her beautiful face. Not wanting to hear the words behind the look, still I asked, "Were you speaking to me?"

She replied, "I said it's you who are the cause of our not having *koinonia*. It came to me so clearly today in the lecture. It's all your fault."

I was too stunned to speak back. I simply jumped from my chair, bolted from that room to my own, and locked the door behind me.

This crisis taught me that the incarnate community (the true primary group, the Christian fellowship) will be small and will not exist for itself. Individual development, growth, and participation will be only one central focus of the whole. At the same time the entire community is urging each individual to become a whole (holy) and participating member, not only of the community itself but of the larger society of which it is part, the individual member will, in learning to become her true self, become a cooperative member of the smaller community. This also is part of the essence of true womanhood.

The woman who does not know herself is not free and open but is uncooperative, selfish, withdrawn (or the reverse, too mannish and domineering). The woman who comes to wholeness through learning to know who she is soon comes to know what her role in life is. Her role as a whole woman is to embrace the world, to love it with all its paradoxes. The great opposites— beauty and ugliness, light and dark, joy and sorrow, pain and pleasure, bound and free, male and female—will be stabilized within her new understanding of her destiny as woman. Her role is to bear within her, as though pregnant, the seeds of all these opposites; to accept the mystery of what will be nurtured within her as she accepts herself, other people, and the reality of her own existence and her own environment. The woman whose basic thrust is toward living a religious life will be increasingly willing and eager to be the "handmaid of the Lord," even as the growing reality of her holiness grips her and causes her to be "greatly disturbed," as Christ's own mother was at a similar juncture in her life (see Luke 1:26-35).

While we help one another individually to become more and more whole in small communities, we must at the same time avoid in every way possible investing our newfound wholeness and humanity in the community itself. If we do, we will become introverted and sick individually and as a community. Instead, at the same time we learn in openness and trust to help and support one another toward a new maturity, we should keep our eye on growing service through open relationships to persons outside the community and on global health. This openness to the outside allows for further growth within both individuals and community.

Whether or not we are aware of it, we have come into an age

of the corporate personality. Our world desperately needs every Christian to become visible in some form of loving community where each member is making the effort to become honest, where people can see us living and working together in freedom and love. This openness to one another will emanate from our openness to the Spirit of God.

Jesus gave us the foretaste of this by gathering around him trusted disciples and friends whom he loved and with whom he was open. He said once to his disciples: I am your friend because I have told you everything that the Father has told me; the servant does not know what the master is doing, but the friend who does what God commands does know what the friend is doing (see John 15:14-16). He gives this message not to one disciple, but to all. As he trained the disciples he made it clear that they should not go alone on their missions but should go by twos and stay in the homes of people who accepted them. He recognized our need for one another, and this added power and trust which comes through association with those who hold the same basic beliefs. Jesus also knew that a religion which stays to itself is quickly perverted and often perverts the persons involved in it.

The entire process of growth, both individually and corporately, is massively painful. But we cannot expect the joy of life or a celebrative spirit without pain and discipline.

Jesus moved calmly through all the brutality, the rejection, the blood and sweat and tears. But this, as we know, was not the end of the story. His obedience to doing the difficult task, his participation in the difficult event, and his belief that God would see him though regardless of how bad things looked resulted in life and joy, celebration and glory.

I have high hope and great faith in the single woman. She is capable of so much more than she knows, both for her own benefit and for others. But she must be awakened, she must act, she must share her life. And she must be willing to take the first step.

part II

LIFE STORY

CHAPTER 10

A Night of Despair

This book witnesses to the conviction that there is a force beckoning you and me into fuller life. No matter what your age or marital status, your race, religion, color, creed, political affiliation, economic level, or sex, this loving reality beckons you forward into abundant, joyous life here and now. But because human beings make wrong choices, are resistant to change, and are, more often than not, taught distorted concepts, they become aware of this gracious force only after all else has failed.

All else had failed for me in 1956 at the age of thirty-seven. My marriage had ended in a dramatic and soul-wrenching series of misunderstandings and unwillingnesses of both parties to listen to the other. Now I was driving from the east coast to my mother's home in Chicago in a fog of pain and misery.

Suddenly three screams pierced the shadows of night—long, wailing cries. Silence. Ages later, sobs pushed themselves up through the despair and shook my frame. Then, again, silence. The silence was more real than the sobs, more pregnant than the deep, black night about me. My inner being stirred to its call.

"You out there in the blackness, are you there? Is my belief that you are dead a lie? Shall I give you a chance—the only chance I have left?"

And the stillness answered not a word. The car droned on while the night continued to chain me in blackness.

"*Do* something, will you? Everywhere I turn I make a mess of things. I need someone to take over. Will you do it? Please help me! Are you there?"

Slowly, so slowly, my sobs subsided. My weary body was drained

of emotion; it longed for rest. As I began to search for a place
to pull off the road, chilling thoughts of what could happen to a
woman so situated late at night, coupled with inner anxiety, forced
me to keep driving. My destination lay six hours ahead.

Six hours! As I pressed on my very real problems began to reveal themselves, tumbling about in my mind, seeking outward
expression.

Too many crisis points in life. Too many failures. Every cell of
my being seemed to scream out at the chaos within, at the lack
of understanding of the important persons in my life, at the lop-
sidedness of justice. For thirty-seven years I had tried to be "a
good girl." All my conscious efforts had been turned toward doing the things I thought others expected of me or wanted me to
do. Though none of it had worked out as I had thought it would
or had wanted it to, I had tried to be a good daughter, a good
wife, a successful worker. But I had failed miserably in all these
relationships. Why?

From the mass of chaos my mind picked up the word success.
What did this word really mean? Most people pressed to be a
success in some area of life. What did success have to do with life
itself? What did it have to do with happiness and contentment, of
which I had none?

Or had I ever been a success? I had graduated with high hon-
ors from both high school and college—was that success, as my
family thought? I was pretty and had played the role of the typi-
cal girl of my time and place. Popularity banged on my door. I
turned more dates down than I accepted. My father and my peers
were proud of me. But the more popularity I had, the more dead
and hollow I felt inside. Was popularity success? My friends
seemed to think so. Who was right?

In whatever work I did there were always advancements. I
was conscientious, pouring my soul into each new endeavor only
to become bored and empty. But I made more and more money,
and my bosses and co-workers thought I had done quite well.
Working day and night, traveling, being always on the go kept

me from analyzing why there was a rising flood of anger, anxiety, and fear inside me.

What had gone wrong, that dissatisfaction rather than a sense of completion filled my days? In extracurricular activities I was in demand; organization and planning were easy for me. I was efficient and clever, worked hard, and my masks had smiles on them. People liked to have me around because I got the job done. They used to say, "I just don't know how you do it! You're never idle—always on the go. When do you sleep?" No one, least of all myself, ever thought to ask, "When do you have time to form a fulfilling relationship?" No, the theme was: make money, be popular, marry young, be successful. But was success to be measured by popularity and efficiency?

How then, when I seemed to be fulfilling society's expectations, had I reached this ultimate crisis point? Why do I say ultimate? Because whatever happened now meant literally either life or death. I sensed this; I could not verbalize it. This was a great moment in my personal history. The crossroads had been reached, and I had to ask myself new questions. Unfortunately, nothing had prepared me for such a moment.

The whirling thoughts and questions settled momentarily, and I drove in utter silence for several more miles. Had I ever been truly silent before? Like one parched with thirst, my body and soul drank silence in. My body, which moments before had seemed lifeless with its weight of worry and fear, began to stir at the sight of outlines of trees and mountains spread against the black sky. The car light penetrated the vast darkness, picking out small night animals, bushes, rocks.

Little Penny, my dog, stirred in my lap—she was a five-pound toy fox terrier who had been my constant companion for two years. I wasn't grateful for much on that ride—I had not been grateful for much for a long time—but I know now that that little dog kept me in touch with reality. Looking at her I thought of what Henry Drummond had written: "It is when a man has no one to love him that he commits suicide. So long as he has friends, those who love him and whom he loves, he will live; because to live is to love. If it is but the love of a dog, it will keep him in life; but let that go and he has no contact with life, no reason to live."

I turned my attention from the road as the dog stirred and quieted her with a stroke, wondering why human relationships could not be as simple as the relationship with one's dog. It was a long time before I was to know the real answer to this.

But now the restlessness would not leave me alone.

"You are a failure. You have failed in your marriage and in all your human relationships. You are scared and full of self-pity. How did you get yourself in this mess?"

"I suppose because I am scared and full of self-pity."

"But why are you so self-pitying? You just said everyone thought you were doing quite well."

"On the surface I am. But there's such a gap between the surface and the reality. I'm not sure who I am, where I'm going, or why I'm living. I'm confused. Everything seems futile; there's no meaning in anything I do."

Yes, until recently the surface had looked good. The average woman might easily have envied the picture I presented so far as looks, position, money, and accomplishments were concerned. Yet here I was, driven by fear, indecision, resentment, failure. Under the outward poise I felt the pressure of too many demands, and no one seemed to like or understand me. I was in a turmoil, contemplating my failures and distributing the blame for them over many people. I was then incapable of realizing that many of my feelings and attitudes came about through my own choices.

Three hours to go . . . and then Chicago.

Weariness slipped away as my life flashed before me.

CHAPTER 11

Wrong Choices

I was a sensitive, intelligent child who tried to pretend all was well with my parents, though it was not. I was shuffled from father to mother to grandparents and back again until my parents made a final break when I was about sixteen. During those years of being moved about I had erected many scruples against drinking and other "moral sins." I was reluctant to admit that my father, whom I adored, was an old pro in all aspects of the seamy side of life. He was a sadist. My mother was demanding and moralistic.

Through those formative years both parents had expected the best of me—scholastically, socially, morally. I could never have measured up.

The inevitable pattern of drifting into trying to please my peers, since I was unable to please my parents, led me to marry at age twenty, a college dropout. At twenty-two I lost my baby, and two years later my husband died a sudden and tragic death.

Now, a quarter-century after these events, I recognize that much of the trauma of those years could not be traced to those two deaths. The true drama was played out in the pain which is always the result of children attempting to play house in grown-up bodies. Because I had not grown up I was not aware of my own identity. Not knowing who I was made it impossible to know what it means to be a woman. The further fact that I was intelligent and somewhat talented masked the reality and complicated the misery.

My husband, Garland, filled the prescription of all the magazine advertisements. He really was tall (6'4"), had dark hair and eyes, and was very handsome. He had a good sense of humor, was a pleasant host, and danced well. He asked me to marry him on our first date, and I asked no questions. My marriage was a romantic, swirling flutter of excitement. At last I would have a home and understanding, thought I, and I wanted a dozen children. But I, an only child who had never had many playmates, was not prepared for the avalanche of my husband's ten brothers and sisters married to ten other people, each couple with children of its own. In this large family (almost fifty in all) no one took anyone else very seriously. Because I was still a child, and an only one at that, I demanded attention. Not receiving it, I felt lost and alone. Besides, it may be true that women need persons more than men do. I know only that life was misery and loneliness, and the warm body of a man could not make up for all the elements which were missing in our communication with one another.

Reason and justice, it seems to me, would dictate that married persons who cannot or do not have a true relationship should not be able to have babies of their own. But life does not flow on such a smooth course, and so I became pregnant.

For the first few days I was in a flutter of excitement, but soon the responsibilities began to loom large and overcome the anticipation. The conflict of happiness and dread further delayed any understanding my husband and I may have had of our situation.

The child part of my nature demanded more and more attention from my husband, who tried to give it to me. He had put me on a pedestal from the beginning, and now that I was to bear his child he adored and worshiped me. But the more he tried to love me in this manner the more dissatisfied and demanding I became. Neither of us had a glimpse of the cause of our plight. My real need was to be treated as a person, not as a toy to be idolized. His need was for a real woman who could forget herself in order to embrace him fully.

Still, we were like two children looking forward to a third;

and so moments of fun and gay anticipation were interspersed between the moments of pain.

In the seventh month I hemorrhaged, and my waterbag broke. After six weeks, as I lay flat on my back with around-the-clock care, the child came into the world stillborn. During those six weeks my husband and I grew farther and farther apart. Since the relationship was built on physical appetite and dreams, it now had little to sustain it. Hour after hour, day in and day out, I lay looking at the ceiling and pushing in the anger and frustration I felt. Increasingly, the boy-man worked late and stopped off for drinks with his buddies. He berated himself for my condition and escaped the responsibility of being a husband and a man in every way he could find.

I was now too crushed and scared to demand. I longed for him to talk with me or simply to sit long enough for me to talk with him, but he could not bear the pain. My silent anger and frustration turned to hostility and resentment. I swore to avenge myself once I got out of that bed. He was proud of the fact that I didn't drink, and I hated drinking to excess. Still, I'd prove to him I could drink as well and as much as any of his friends. In some dark corner of my mind I must have felt such action would bring me the desired and longed-for companionship.

Anger and frustration piled itself higher upon the old anger and frustration at the birth of our child. Though it was passé, I had wanted very much to have a normal childbirth—without drugs. In spite of the fear which had been generated during the six-week illness, I wanted to taste and feel and experience this great miracle of giving birth. It seemed to me so much more human and loving for a woman to be a full participant in the entire event. It somehow seemed inhuman that my husband could not be with me and that we both were not as involved and aware as possible of the arrival of our child.

The doctor was late arriving. It appeared that the longer we waited the nearer the entire staff came to a state of panic. Or was this my own reaction? At one high point of fear I must have

cried out, for immediately a nurse was at my side with a glass
of water and a pill. When she admitted it was something that
would reduce the pain I begged her to allow me the privilege of
experiencing everything. She went away and returned with what
appeared to be a glass of water. This I eagerly drank, but soon
became aware that she had duped me and that the water had
contained the hated pill. I felt cheated, deprived.

Now a hazy fog set in. People came and went as though in a
dream sequence. On occasion a face stood out in high or bas-
relief from the haze or a voice penetrated it, and these are etched
forever in my memory.

The first sound I heard was the voice of my husband asking
if my father and his paramour could visit. Demons seemed to
descend through the fog. Why bother me at a time like this with
such a complex affair? My mother attended me, and now my
sadistic father and his mistress wished to join her. I don't know
what I answered, but mercifully the mist turned to deep black,
and I floated on a featherbed of drugs to obvilion.

Later I heard voices that sounded as though they were far out
at sea, voices that floated to me on an icy air. A man's face
thrust itself through the mist, and the faraway voice said, "Everything will be all right now."

"Is it a boy?" I asked. "Is he alive?"

"Yes, it's a boy."

And my insides quavered. Something deep, *deep* within
warned me that my boy was dead. Anger at that man's half-
truth settled itself on my heart. It was to be twenty years before
it was to be overcome. During those twenty years this inner rage
took a heavy toll on my personality, my health, my willingness
to live.

But now I was immersed in the fog again, floating away to a
dazzlingly beautiful island. I shall never forget that island. I'm
certain it gave me a foretaste of the glory of eternal life. Looking
back, I marvel that I was not changed on the spot to a loving
creature. But the anger had already attached itself to my heart,

and the school of life is not that pat or that lacking in challenge and adventure.

Some hours later I awakened to a bright, midafternoon, early-August heat. My father and his mistress had arrived. I was subjected not only to the stifling heat, my own perspiration, and the awful wonderment concerning our dead child but to the bickering of the family from which my mother had tried to shield me. Consciousness came and went for several hours before a severe fever hit and the blessed fog settled around me once again.

I cried to go to the island and found myself unable to approach it, though it lay in the distance, beckoning. Now the haze was filled with many faces of both friend and foe. They were tossed about like balloons in a high wind. I was a balloon also—twisting, turning, running, searching—searching for love, for understanding, for someone who would see me as a person. But each balloon-face saw in me what it could get from me: one wanted to fulfill his own identity through mine; another wished only my participation in the sex act; another desired the efficiency and conscientiousness I brought to my work; another longed to vent his rage upon me. I became afraid and tried to scream.

A hand reached down and stuck a hard piece of wood between my teeth. A green canopy covered me. I saw not a soul—only the hairy hand.

Blackness descended.

Days later I was told that the green canopy had been an oxygen tent and that I had experienced a mortal struggle in which life had won over death.

They took me home a more bitter person. Why had I not been allowed to go to the island? Surely the baby was there.

I kept all these deadly things and pondered them in my heart. They were not the thoughts and feelings which build up and make strong, but they did contribute to making me more aggressive and domineering.

For the next fifteen months my husband and I ran from life. We laughed and partied and drank. We moved to California to get away from the memories, only to find they followed us. We were in San Diego when Pearl Harbor was announced, and soon my husband's draft call arrived. We moved back to the Midwest and I was left alone while he entered basic training. He was later stationed in Louisiana, where I joined him and where a freak and tragic accident took his life.

The searing pain of abandonment and loneliness from this double loss convinced me that God was dead, or that if he lived, he loved me not. I was without a compass and filled with the anguish of guilt and disbelief. I wanted to be with my mother. It was summer 1943.

In late 1944, Mother (who worked as a nurse in Chicago) and I decided to pool our assets toward the purchase of a house in order to accommodate as economically as possible ourselves, mother's father and sister, and Mary, a friend of mine. We were in new surroundings, without friends beyond our small world. We were an aimless crew with little purpose in life other than our daily jobs. Grandfather was a proud old patriarch who found taking orders from younger women distasteful and irritating. Aunt Fern had been crippled from childhood by polio. Her job, a thankless one I fear, was to do the housework for the rest of us. The brace on her leg and arthritis caused her a great deal of pain which she bore stoically. This attitude often made her seem indifferent, though in truth she was not. She resented what she felt was her narrow life and seldom entered into family decisions. Mother worked long, hard days and nights with irascible patients. She came home weary and burdened. A recent operation had added to her general despondency, her self-pity, and her sense of guilt. She had an unusually difficult time communicating her feelings. Soon she became short-tempered and irritable. And it's obvious that I myself reached this stage in life with little hope and much despair.

Of all of us, Mary was the most calm. She and I lived for pretty clothes and the hope of a date. But the war was at its peak, and there were few men available.

We were sitting on a powder keg of anger, fear, and boredom. Words were said, conversations happened, there was, on occasion, real fun and laughter. But although there were all the proper manifestations of normal involvement, disintegration was taking place in and around me. We lived together ambivalently —hating each other, needing each other, loving each other. We seldom communicated at depth; we seldom made contact.

It was at this point that the confusion and sense of alienation from self, from God, from family was so great that I succumbed to my mother's projection of her own enslavement and sought the help of a psychiatrist. The insight he gave me about my excessively strong superego which would not leave me in peace seemed only to create in me greater confusion and unhappiness. My body experienced the physical pain that only a tormented spirit can create—headaches and various bowel and stomach troubles were not the least of this reaction.

When the doctor employed by the agency for which I worked recognized that the source of my symptoms was not physical, he asked me what I wanted most in life to do. On discovering that I longed to continue my education, he recommended that I waste no time in returning to college. His offer to help me gain admission is one of the most meaningful recollections of this period of my life. This man not only planted an idea in my head, he helped me to pursue it. Studying distracted me from what by this time had become a morbid preoccuption—reading books and magazine articles about psychoanalysis and psychology. The view I had acquired of myself as a result of this reading was far more ugly and impossible than the reality. I did not know this then. I did not know it because there was no one to help me affirm or deny the things I was learning about myself and life.

Authentic, life-giving questions seemed to be an affront to friends and ministers alike. I began to discover that most people are unable to discuss themselves openly and honestly. No one I met at that period of life seemed willing to expose himself to the questions I was asking—questions about God, the Bible, life itself. "If death is an absolute, why am I on earth?" "What am I to do that no one else can do by virtue of who I am?" "Who am I?" "Why am I this person instead of that person? And what does this difference mean in the total scheme of things?" "Is my life really important? If it is, how and why am I failing so miserably in relationships with my family and friends?" "Why do I feel so hopeless, and why is life so meaningless?"

These and many other questions were pushed deep within for want of anyone with whom to discuss them. Had I known then the damage this repression would cause, I might have fought harder to find answers.

At the time of graduation I turned down a splendid fellowship at a top university because a professor made me feel that I would become ugly and hard if I were to continue my education. His remark that fateful day when I went for advice was, "A woman like you should be married. If you go for your Ph.D. in zoology you will come to look like the specimens you work on—and who will want you then?"

This remark had deep consequences in my life for a long time. Not only did I delay graduate work for eighteen years (and it might very well have been forever), I worried about the remark in both its aspects: Why didn't I get married, and why hadn't I gone ahead with my education? Why had I listened to that professor? *Because he was a man,* and it was expected that a woman would listen to a man. In some perverse way his destructive remark seemed like a compliment, yet it created within me uncertainty and disillusionment. There was no one to help me see how I was almost to destroy myself by not using and developing my talents.

In 1948 I graduated and began a process of moving from one good job to a better one, always keeping busy at outside activities. I seemed to be drifting along on the edge of life—a life which more and more threatened to hurl me into a black abyss.

The men I met had little or no understanding of the need a woman has to be a person, and not a plaything or just a thing.

I began to hate myself for being only a body and to long for someone, particularly a man, with whom I could have an intelligent conversation and who would at least try to understand my need for identification—for being accepted as I was and for what I might be able to become. Successive failures to establish communication with men or women at a level that would bring to me serenity in place of temporary distraction became so stark that I was convinced that *single persons should be given far more attention by church and society.* I discovered there were many single persons like myself who were without a guide, a stay, a rudder, a direction.

Although my experience with the church was practically nonexistent at this time, the yearning to participate in something meaningful pressed me forward. Visits to two pastors who were uninterested and one who actually laughed in my face were enough, in the weakened state of my ego, to discourage me. The only response these pastors could produce was to "turn the church into a marriage bureau." But my experience indicated that this was not the answer.

Not knowing what else to do, I threw myself into ceaseless activity. Seldom getting proper food and rest, I became more and more fatigued with the constant though unconscious drive to excel. Anxiety accentuated my faults, and I became increasingly aggressive and domineering. Under the charm and outer poise there crouched a fierce hostility and bitterness against man and God. The backwash of wretchedness created a longing to escape. I began to drink and date a great deal. The drinks cut the edge of the crass expectations of boys in men's bodies. It was almost as though the frustrated urge to flee by means of the sexual act had become a venomous urge to flail one another, and finally a hidden urge to kill one another.

Most of the women I knew were married, and even though few of them were happy they began to push me toward matrimony. Everyone seemed to feel it was a little odd that I didn't marry. Finally, ten years after the death of my first husband, I married again. This was not a mature decision. It was made because of my loneliness, which bordered on desperation, and because of the pressures of society.

Unfortunately, sex was the substitute for intimacy in this second marriage, and the union became saddled with demands it could not meet.

Ten years of experience, the academic subjects I had pursued, the psychotherapy I had undergone, had not changed the ambivalent and demanding child of my past. Worse, this time I had married my father. Not literally, of course, but this man had the sadistic tendencies I had become accustomed to in my youth.

My husband was no more mature than I. He hated his mother and therefore me. Ours was a "Virginia Woolf marriage." Indifference and late hours at work or with his buddies were my husband's attempts to say I was not acting like a real woman and that he was miserable and needed love. Exaggerating inconsequential matters, pouting, and being demanding of his time were my ways of saying that I was in agony because he was not more a man. We both drank and shouted at one another and used sex as a weapon.

The situation became so intolerable that I twice attempted suicide. But these desperate bids for attention and understanding netted nothing more than deeper distaste, distrust, and contempt from my husband.

Looking back, it is easy for me to see that the affectional ties of sex are not enough to foster the ends of a mutually satisfactory companionship in marriage; sex is only one of the many channels through which mutuality can be built up. Because the marriage had no other medium through which we could broaden ourselves, our weaknesses were intensified. Because neither one would or even could listen to the cries of the other, both felt isolated and alone. His immature cruelty increased while my immature hostility went rampant.

We were both in need of loving someone, but we didn't know how. With neither of us able to give or receive love that had any identification with anything beyond the physical act, it still took four years for the marriage to disintegrate.

It was at the end of this second marriage that I found myself in the car, pressing through a black night that symbolized the darkness of my soul, with Penny on my lap. Dawn was stealing over the Chicago skyline before I had finally admitted I could not save myself. I knew I needed help.

CHAPTER 12

The Turning Point

Grandfather had died in 1954, and my friend Mary had long since left the home which my mother and aunt now shared. Mother had undergone two serious operations which apparently had had a debilitating influence on her will to recover. She was only fifty-nine, but had lain down to die. Life, it seemed, had been too cruel.

The nightmare of my soul was my mother's nightmare too. I knew this now. I knew, too, that the guilt we both felt because of our inability to save the other the pain and hurt of past years was where our alliance began. We loved each other, but between us the walls that separated us spiritually grew higher and higher. If I could not save myself, I could not save Mother. To put it another way: until I found my own inner identity I could not allow her the freedom to be what she wanted to be.

The agony of this truth transferred itself into bad dreams which continued to haunt me during the day. There was no healthy slumber for surcease, nor could I permit myself the luxury of the escape the barbiturates tendered my mother. However many times I was weak in other respects, the hope for life was strong enough still in me to resist such remedies for despair. I do not mean to imply that I never considered taking my own life, but I would not choose death through slow disintegration.

It was this very adversity which settled itself in our midst that was responsible for prodding me toward the light of spiritual freedom. But I was still running from the realities that would eventually free me. I often worked eighteen hours a day and drove my weary body to late-night activities as well. I didn't think it out at the time, but I must have felt that if I could just keep busy and do enough "good deeds" I could keep others—and myself—from the real me.

I was *afraid* of the real me, whom I saw as aggressive and cold (everyone knows a feminine being should be soft and cuddly and warm); as critical of others (a "lady" should never take the initiative, should let the man do so, if there is one, or someone "out there" be prominent in decision-making); as hating and hateful (a real lady is never angry, always sweet and kind). Yes, I was afraid of this me, and perhaps I threw myself into good deeds so as never to see her.

The errors of my ways, my failures, my inability to communicate in love with persons continued to eat like acid into the center of my being. I longed to turn my mind off, for it seemed incapable of leaving the vicious circle of self-pity, self-hatred, self-concern in which it continually revolved. I struggled to escape the pit this circular motion was forming. My muscles were taut as though waiting for some further blow. There were many times when I felt as though my body would blow up, if my mind did not.

Forgiveness

In the midst of this dark whirlpool came a shaft of light. Dr. Colin Williams, now of Yale University, had come to our vicinity to give a series of lectures on the parables of Jesus. The fourth in the series was the story of the prodigal son (Luke 15:11-32). I identified with what Dr. Williams said about the younger son who "took his journey into a far country, and . . . squandered his property in loose living." This son had become a daughter, and I was that daughter. "And when she had spent everything, a great famine arose in that country, and she began to be in want. So she went and joined herself to one of the citizens of that country, who sent her into his field to feed swine. And she would gladly have fed on the pods that the swine ate; and no one gave her anything." I saw that there was a great famine in my own soul and heart, and that was why I was in this state of yearning to discover the meaning of life and to have true communication with some other human being and with God the Father.

Who were these citizens who sent me among the swine? Were they to be identified with my own wrong choices—the choices toward death rather than toward life? Were they separate and distinct individuals, or were they representative of a mass social milieu which had the wrong answers or no answers to the questions of my seeking soul? I decided each aspect had played its part in the drama of my life.

Bring the fatted calf and kill it, and let us eat and make merry; for this my daughter was dead, and is alive again; she was lost, and is found. Is it possible, I wondered, that this meant complete forgiveness without recriminations, without judgment? Another part of me rejected the thought because it seemed too fantastic, too impossible. Unconditional forgiveness? Whoever heard of such a thing?

Stunned with the force of the concept, I simply sat for some minutes without conscious thought. Then I felt my hand go up, unbidden, and my voice blurted out, "But, Dr. Williams, how many times can one be forgiven?"

His eyes searched mine for a flash second, then firmly but compassionately he answered, "Seventy times seven (Matt. 18:22)."

There was authority in the remark, an authority I could not escape. I knew irreversibly that the sons and daughters of the Father are loved because they are forgiven unconditionally. *I* was forgiven and *I* was loved. An unnameable elation seemed to well up from deep within me, and I felt the first hint of that true peace which is beyond description.

I was not instantly made whole. A great struggle between those citizens who sent me out among the swine and those who forgave "seventy times seven" followed.

Disillusionment with the Church

Since some of my questions were beginning to be answered I now had the courage to move away from my mother and little dog Penny. I accepted a job as secretary-manager at a church camp, but continued to run from facing the reality of my inner life.

This was my introduction to the institutional church, and because by this time I had determined that the course I must follow was to be a spiritual one, in light of my previous failures to obtain the inner serenity I sought, this opportunity to work with ministers seemed like a true answer to my prayers.

I entered then into the new job with zest and enthusiasm and felt assured of finding Christian community. The disillusionment that followed was simply another rung down the ladder to hell. Of the team of four ministers I came to know, one turned out to have orientation in the spiritual realm. The others were simply businessmen with the ability to maneuver people under the guise of the cloth. I was caught between this disproportionate representation of spirit and materialism, and I was helpless to extricate myself gracefully from the complex politics that emerged.

I cried out for justice and understanding, but I accomplished nothing other than alienating further those around me. Crushed and desperate for help, I searched my memory for just one human being who might help me understand the diabolical nature of the situation in which I found myself—someone who could help me make some order of the chaos both within me and without. Such a person had participated in a family session at our camp. He had shown openness, interest in others, and a commitment to values higher than any I had ever experienced. He had inspired me. He had appeared to like me. Maybe he could help.

When I called, his response was one of complete attention to my need and understanding concerning the church situation. Willis E. Elliott helped me to see that even though my actions and thoughts had often been wrong, still the basic problem resided elsewhere than with me. This note of confidence in me and in my intentions gave me a thin ray of hope. At long last I began seriously and with purpose to put things right with myself.

Beginning of a New Life

When I left the church camp I decided to seek out a retreat where I might in some way find the answers, which I compulsively sought, to the questions swirling in the whirlpool of my existence.

The retreat center was located near the city where I had lived with my first husband. The city and the cemetery where my husband and child were buried brought back images of a past dimmed by the smog of many emotional upheavals and disappointments. The people at the retreat received me warmly, and some of the hope that had just been quenched through that institutional-church experience was renewed in the hospitality I found there.

One significant experience was my giving up smoking. I considered smoking bad for my health, but I could not eliminate the habit. A lady at the camp suggested I stop smoking, and she said she would pray for me. I was amazed the next morning to discover I had no desire to smoke. I gave away the carton of cigarettes I had brought with me and have not touched cigarettes since. No doubt about it, this was a miracle. I still regard it as such—not because the outer manifestation of distrust in one's own small universe (the smoking) was removed, but because through this act I was assured that mankind's weak and distorted powers are not the only strength human beings have to rely on. Something "out there" really was working for my good.

After six weeks' rest, during which I had attended some courses of instruction, it was time for me to find another job. By early fall, through an interesting sequence of happenings, I was ensconced as personal secretary to Dr. Elliott, of the Division of

Evangelism of the United Church Board for Homeland Ministries in Cleveland. Dr. and Mrs. Elliott were already familiar with much of my background and were well aware that the inner struggle which wracked my body on occasion must run its course to the bitter end, to the turn in the journey when all old feelings would begin to be made new. In spite of the awareness that to hire me would be a trial for both of them, the two agreed not only to employ me but to nurture and uphold me through the testing and pain they could foresee. This man and this woman welded harmoniously the serious with the joyous, had a sense of the human, and deeply believed in the goodness and mercy of God. And they were willing to put their bodies where their mouths were. They not only voiced compassion and verbally witnessed to God's love, they acted out the compassion and understanding at great cost to themselves. Herein lay my redemption: that they truly loved God and showed it to me.

Second Fetus

My habit was one of overconscientiousness. I seldom missed a day at work and often arrived early and left several hours after everyone else had gone home. Thus when I did not show up for work one day, Dr. Elliott became quite concerned. He called his wife, who instantly responded by coming to my apartment.

Loree Elliott found me curled fetus-shape on the couch of my living room. I knew my body was there as I knew the couch supported it—a thing outside the black, icy-hot cavern of my existence. My friend Loree was there too, but she was outside my outside; and much of the time, though I vaguely felt her presence, I was not consciously aware of it. Several years later, when we discussed this episode, she said I had not screamed at her to go home as I thought I had. She said she had only been aware that something deep within me was grateful for her presence, and so she stayed.

Three forces were trying to influence the fetus I had become, making me unable to accept either my body or the eternal blackness of oblivion where it rested while the forces wrestled for its possession. One was a demanding voice which kept telling me never to get up again; the second was a consistent, kindlier force which urged me to try to talk to my friend; the third seemed to be outside me, strangling, oppressing, keeping my body riveted to the couch.

A bloody war was going on, a war of opposites—a battle for my life. Part of me was embarrassed, for I was certain the neighbors would be disturbed by the shrieking and shouting going on in me. At the same time there was a dynamic silence in the room which was energizing, beckoning me to come forward, to accept the body curled up as though still in my mother's womb. Months later I was to recognize that energizing silence as the Holy Spirit, urging me to come out of the icy-hot blackness into life and light through the prayers of my friend.

The battle raged. It raged for three days, during which I lived constantly in that icy-hot hell. Much of what transpired is now a blank in my memory, washed mercifully away in the months that followed. But I cannot quite forget walking the floor in an anguished sweat at one moment, and the next throwing myself prone on the floor, the bed, the couch, desiring never to rise again.

My mind thrashed outside that body bulk, which in turn thrashed against the furniture and against life. I hated both my body and the life it contained. I wanted it dead so I could be free, but thoughts of my mother and aunt and of my friend praying intervened, and I would be thrown back into my icy-hot cavern. Sometimes I sat staring at nothing, and at other times I cried great, wrenching sobs. Yet again I would sit or walk silently despairing, with hot tears pouring down my cheeks.

Near the end of these three days, which seemed like an eternity to me, Dr. Elliott and Loree both spent an afternoon listening to me, silently praying for me, calling me out of myself. This was a decisive turning point. I turned toward life instead of death.

Loree's silent vigil had aided the kindlier force to gain the upper hand. Slowly, through the weeks ahead, I moved from hating myself to an ambivalent struggle between hate and acceptance, trust and distrust, fear and confidence, pride and humility. Backward and forward the pendulum swung. Coming forward into the light which the love of my newfound friends generated was very painful. Often tears would well up and spill over because it seemed so incredible that someone could really trust me and like me just as I was.

I know now that they had their eye on my potential and not my defects, and thus were able to overlook the outer manifestations of inner conflicts. They waited for me to ask my own questions. Above all, they listened. They listened to what my heart was saying even more than to my words. They did not assume too much, nor did they judge before the fact, nor did they try to inform me or teach me. Both were aware that each of us has within herself her own questions and her own answers to those questions. The ear that listens in love, however, enables the potential in the other to be fulfilled.

Tears

One of the most important things that came out of that first period of growth was these friends' acceptance of my tears. So many times I've recalled those poignant words "Jesus wept (John 11:35)," and have been grateful for the gift of tears. I shed buckets of tears. Had I not been allowed to do so, I'm certain the days of celebration and joy would have been much delayed. I speak not of tears of self-pity, which are signals that one desires attention, but of silent, cleansing tears. As it was, neither of these friends ever once flinched when the tears began to roll. Even at the office there were times when I would be so filled with the changes which are necessary if one is to move from the old woman to the new that tears would flow. I was sorry to embarrass people because of them. But those tears, I now know, were essential to my spiritual health. Later, at a growth group seminar (see pp. 130–35), the tears rolled softly and silently for three days. The retreat leader explained to the group (in an effort to release us all from embarrassment) that even the chemistry is different in these two kinds of tears. I shall always be grateful to that leader for having the insight to let the healing waters flow without interruption. I learned from this experience not to make the silencing statement "Oh, don't feel bad; don't cry," or the silencing question "Will you tell me what is wrong?" It seems to me perverse that anyone should need to feel embarrassed because of tears. Holding back tears creates frustration and anger, which further complicate whatever problems a person has. It also emphasizes the feeling that "nobody understands; nobody cares." On the other hand, because I was accepted tears and all, I was later able to sort out the differences between what appeared to be self-pity and depression from the simple cleansing of anxiety and fear.

During those early days in Cleveland, when I wanted to die, the tears were tears of frustration—a release from the pain of life. Those tears were generally accompanied by a deep, enervating depression. But the cleansing tears allowed me to continue about my daily tasks while my world was taking on new dimensions.

CHAPTER 13

Search for New Values

During this transitional period I was reading *The Seven Deadly Sins* by Lance Webb and lamenting over how many *I* possessed. I wrote down every evil mentioned in the Bible—quite a list! Already weary and disgusted with myself, I only added fuel to the fire of my conflicts and frustrations. In my search for new values most things seemed petty and unimportant. At night, alone, I hated myself with a terrible loathing for what I believed myself to be. This constant battle left me fatigued and debilitated. The person I thought myself to be was childish, hateful, demanding, petty, self-deceitful, jealous, envious, with a spirit of dissension. Reading Galatians 5:19-21 made me feel I would be nothing but hateful, bored, and weary my entire life. Psychologists might describe the phase as masochistic.

My friend Loree had an answer that no one else had been able to offer me. The answer took root because of her love and her real concern that I become free. The action she took in love was to suggest another course—the course of hope.

When I suggested we study *The Seven Deadly Sins,* she suggested that we study the life of Jesus Christ as it relates to persons and to our own reflections, desires, and prayers. That was the most positive and fruitful advice I have ever been given. Loree not only suggested that I study the life of Christ or the Bible, or that I look into my own reactions and reflections, or that I scrutinize my relationships with others, but that I do all three at once. She was gently leading me away from a concentration on the negative—sin—to positive precepts of trust and love.

As I turned from the degraded and hopeless person I thought

I was to the hope that is in Jesus Christ, my relationship with my brothers and sisters began to free me for hope—the hope which, when pursued, leads to joy and peace. With the release of tension and frustration through having persons who understood and respected me as a person, who were pointing me toward hope, trust, and love, I was enabled to receive new insights into the meaning of life. In the beginning they came one at a time, and as my mind and body assimilated and made use of the new truth I was strengthened to continue the search for further health and truth. Most often what came to me was not so much a completely new thought but rather some idea or concept as old as time, affirmed in the center of my being. No longer did I wonder or think about spiritual matters—now I *knew*. But the knowing was a paradox, for with it came a change in attitude toward having to know. In other words, where formerly I had been insistent on persons hearing me because of inner fear that I did *not* know, now certainty was at my center and I could more easily listen without insisting that the other person hear me. The more completely I could assimilate and integrate the truth within myself, the less I needed to say about it.

My journey now led me through a period of high adventure. I became aware that gratitude and thanksgiving were necessary ingredients for the gift of joy, and that I had lived less than half a life in my ignorance concerning prayer. Repentance, confession, and restitution changed from being dark and threatening words to becoming the necessary ingredients to well-being.

Unity and Wholeness

These new concepts became reality in a series of outward and upward movements, which at a backward glance are so integrated that it is difficult to extricate the parts without destroying the feeling of unity and wholeness which was the outcome.

Over the next three years, my mind, heart, and soul were flooded with the answers I had been seeking for so long. The more

I sought and yearned to find some meaning in existence and purpose for my life, the more widely the door of life was opened. Love, knowledge, healing, forgiveness, integrative experiences of joy and peace rushed to fill the void in my yearning soul. The best way I can find to describe these overlapping experiences is to take each major new experience and deal with it over the period of three years.

MY BODY

Quite early it became clear that, if I were to seek growth in the spirit, all aspects of life must be included. I discovered my body was so closely related to my psyche (soul), mind, and emotions that any one of these carriers of energy could act as a barometer for the others. When I had a migraine headache it was not enough simply to take a pill or a shot of some pain-killer, for the headaches always returned. I began to observe what I was thinking and feeling before a migraine attack. Gradually, I came to be able to bear the pain without medication. As I observed what mind, emotions, and body were doing to one another I was able to name the demon which laid me low.

Every woman has her own demons, but in my case it was anger masked in confusion, the end result of which was the isolated feeling of worthlessness: a conviction that *no one loved me*. By devious evasions I hid from myself the deep hostility I held toward certain important persons in my life, and the fact that it was I who was incapable of love.

When I was finally able to deal honestly and openly with this anger by confessing it existed, by adopting a repentant attitude concerning the hurts I had caused others, by forgiving other persons for the ways in which they had hurt me, by accepting the forgiveness Christ offered me, and by making restitution in various ways, the migraines left—never to return. My thoughts, feelings, and spirit were so closely united with my body that no one aspect could function without the others being vitally involved, whether for good or for ill.

How very grateful I've been for the doctor who took away my pills: the dexedrine, the phenobarb, the iron pills, the pills for gas and the others for constipation. My time had been spent watching the clock to see when I took the next one of the twelve pills I was to consume each day. Each of these pills seemed necessary simply because I would not face the truth that I was an unloving, unrepentant, domineering woman who felt sorry for herself and would not let go.

The words "let go" here mean a great deal more than just letting go of old attitudes and habits. The sleep and pep medicines were necessary because I would not let go of my fears, waste products of an ill-at-ease spirit that were preventing sleep; the pills for gas and constipation were necessary because I wouldn't let go of the waste products of the body (my colon constricts and refuses to let waste pass when my spirit is in rebellion); the iron was necessary to build my blood, which was impoverished by my distorted emotions.

When the doctor took away the medicine and said, "Now you are going to be terribly depressed for a couple of weeks, but you can take it," I began to let go. The cleaner my body became as the alien chemicals were eliminated, the better able I was to let go, to sleep, and to have bowel movements. In letting go in these ways I became less tense and therefore less demanding.

Middle age. The middle age crisis had actually begun for me several months before I went to work for Dr. Elliott. My light blue moods became heavy, dark moods. I was depressed and weepy most of the time. Tears would fly to the surface over practically nothing, and often I would awake crying in the early morning. My outlook on life changed from one of relative optimism to a critical, jealous, selfish, angry attitude. It seemed to me that everyone was against me and there was no justice in the world for *me*.

My insatiable appetite began to take on physical form. I gained thirty pounds in a matter of weeks, my tissues became spongy and watery, and my abdomen would bloat to an embarrassing and painful degree. Sometimes the bloating would be so exaggerated it would push against my heart, causing a choking sensation and fear that I might be having a heart attack.

What zest for living I had formerly had seemed to be lost, and small matters annoyed me inordinately. Where formerly I had always slept well, even with a bad conscience, now I slept fitfully and often not at all. My legs and arms would tingle during the night, and my ears would ring during the day.

I began to look ugly. Not only had the extra weight made me feel out of it, but my face was beginning to look haggard and lined. I was on a treadmill: the worse I felt, the worse I looked, the less I seemed to be able to do about it, and the more I hated myself and my life.

These bodily changes were unnecessarily frightening for me for three reasons. First, I had reached middle age without having worked through my childhood or adolescent crisis, so the crisis of middle age became almost, if not completely, intolerable.* The second reason apprehensions had reached such mammoth proportions was that I had heard so many women talk about "change-of-life melancholia," the fear of going insane, apprehension that they might now get cancer or heart trouble. Women who had not faced reality before menopause called up all sorts of weird fantasies which did nothing more than assist them in fulfilling their fears.

The third reason I felt more confused and frightened than necessary in menopause was that most doctors are men, and only the rare male doctor can truly understand the inner turmoil, the feelings of uselessness and unworthiness, the actual physical pain a woman often endures. I had gone to several doctors who only increased in me feelings of ugliness and fear. When I described my symptoms they asked how old I was and then brushed everything aside with, "Oh, you're just experiencing some of the

---

* The writings of Erik Erikson, on unfinished business from the earlier of the eight life-stages, are particularly instructive on this. See his *Childhood and Society.*

changes of menopause." The words alone were not crushing, but the attitude of superiority and indifference served to do nothing but increase all my problems. I commented to the Elliotts, "Doctors treat a woman like a hunk of meat, not like a person. I feel like one of their lab specimens."

One day at the office, as I was struggling to catch my breath, one of the secretaries insisted on calling a doctor. I pleaded with her not to do so. "Doctors give you no help, no encouragement; they take your money and send you from the office feeling more helpless and dejected than ever," I said. But this time I was fortunate. That doctor really understood. He took time to explain what was going on, what happens to a woman's body during this physiological change, and what she herself can do about it.

When I asked him about shots or pills he said to me, "You can start such medication if you wish. I can take your money without any effort on my part, since my nurse will be the one to see you. But I am an old man and I've treated many women. Let me tell you that it takes only two years, a little more or a little less, for the body to complete its changes. You may have some hot flushes [flashes] now and then, and on occasion some stress and pain. But if you are willing to suffer a little discomfort there's a possibility that menopause will be shortened." Kindly and patiently he explained that the major aspects of this stage of life include the cessation of menstruation, the hot flashes, hormonal change, and some emotional stress.

He suggested that one key to the problem of menopause is the realization and acceptance that it is a normal part of living—something that happens to every woman. The second key is acceptance and affirmation of aging itself. "The sooner you accept it the quicker you can get on to the more important job of living," said he. Once a woman adopts an attitude of affirmation she usually does not seek elaborate treatments and is much more content to experience the symptoms which are inevitable in the aging process.

He concluded by suggesting that if what he advised about not taking medication seemed unrealistic to me after a period of two or three months, I should return to talk with him once again. I left his office with a feeling of hope for the first time in several months. I was not, thankfully, the exceptional woman who needed medication or psychiatric help.

Clothes. The full-length mirror seemed to stretch itself toward me, forcing me to attend to the impression my form made upon it. I started past, not wanting to look; but there I stood before my eyes, appearing exactly as I felt—dejected, frightened, hostile, unhappy. I looked like a has-been in the dull green flat shoes with the heavy soles. The colorless gray dress fit me unbecomingly, and the straight, chopped hair lent nothing of allure to the image. An intensified disgust for what I saw caused me to turn away, but it was already too late to unsee and unfeel the judgment. The mirror-image dogged and jogged my memory by conjuring up before me the evil ghosts of my past, compounded with feeling actual chills in my flesh. I realized then that enlightenment of the spirit is only the beginning; from it begins the slow, uphill climb of accepting the body as castle and home of the soul, so that it truly reflects the nature of the dweller.

After several hours of trying to understand this reaction to the image reflected by the mirror, I returned and tried once more to face the dowdy matron who stared back at me in contempt and skepticism; another skirmish began. She wasn't just stern and unremitting—she was *masculine and harsh.* After a conditional peace of several more hours, the dialogue that took place between my warring natures went like this:

I really should do something about my appearance.

You know that in this new life you are trying to lead material things no longer have priority in your values. Only the egocentric person believes pretty clothes are important. How can you give your all if you are spending time, thought, and money on finery?

But doesn't the outer person reflect the inner one?

· It took some time for the message to penetrate the uppermost reaches of my mind. I didn't like what I was hearing, because what it really meant was that I needed to do a lot of reconstruction work. I was being told I didn't know what I needed to know concerning the meaning of my appearance. Finally I was able to accept that the sallow complexion, the ugly hairdo, the sloppily fitting dress and worker shoes were the outer signs of the aging of mind and body after forty-three years of life together. *Together* we had become gray, old, heavy, done for. These were the obvious signs. There were others also: weariness, metabolism changes with all the manifestations of menopause—hairs appearing in unexpected places on the chin or over the upper lip, and an increase in freckles or moles.

As so often happens when one is working through some conflict, I was soon given an opportunity to test whether or not I meant to do something about my condition. Friends arrived from out of town unexpectedly, and we were to meet for lunch. I dug out my high heels and a string of bright beads to wear with the black skirt and blouse which I wore almost interchangeably with the gray dress, having at that time so little imagination. At our office building, I rode up in the elevator with a man with whom I had worked for eighteen months. I had always felt as though I were offensive to him, but this morning he actually noticed me with a smile. When he left the elevator he said, "You should always wear high heels, you know."

I shall never forget how the warmth, so quickly kindled by a smile, turned into a raging fire of resentment. I was the same person I had been the day before and the day before that. Why should a pair of high heels make so much difference? Would no one ever notice me as a person?

Later I was to recognize that it was not the high heels alone but the happier expression on my face and in my bearing, because I had put on the high heels and the beads, that occasioned the remark. This man had noticed the difference I felt inside. Not to have changed my outer apparel would have (and previously had) concealed the change taking place in me. I came to realize that *the outer person does give good evidence of the inner woman.*

Sex. My personal struggle to place my sexuality in proper perspective began early in my spiritual growth. An overpowering urge to tear at my own flesh awakened me one night. I tossed and turned, holding the feelings and words inside. Shoulder muscles became tense and teeth clenched. I wanted to scream out, "I *need* love, I *need* warmth, I *need* communication beyond the verbal." My entire body ached to be loved, to be held and patted and stroked. Is there any substitute, I wondered, for the warmth of another human being's body touching your own?

I tried turning my thoughts in other directions. If I could only be grateful for the freedoms I have in my single life, I thought. But this is not freedom, to be caught up in such a bondage of desire and frustration! What is this force that makes me want to tear at my own body? Why does it embarrass me to discuss this need? Or is this really a need? Is sex a necessity, or is it a desire? a need, or only a want?

But then how could it be a necessity in the way food, drink, and shelter are? If it were, we would die when we are deprived of it. Yet no one ever dies from the amount of sex one has or doesn't have—one only suffers from one's attitudes about it.

My mind skittered to a contemplation of masturbation, but thinking it a self-centered form of indulgence, I pushed it from my consciousness. I wanted no part in an act which would narrow my world, draw me in on myself, and prevent me from living openly, freely, and joyously.

At last, possibly, I could sleep. I snuggled into the smooth, cool sheets, breathed deeply several times, and tried to relax. But "bugs" crawled up and down my skin. I stretched my muscles, took some more long, deep breaths. But this body which I ignored most of the time would no longer allow my indifference to it; it demanded my attention.

I turned on the light and paced the room. I tried to read. A deeper loneliness set in. An old pattern of thought began to revolve in the whirlpool of my being. "You're getting old (at forty-three) and ugly (this was not true) and done for (not at all—this year of struggle was the beginning of true life)." At that moment nothing could convince me that there was hope in the single state—possibly more hope than in marriage, at least for me.

I decided to take myself in hand. Just how serious is sex, I wondered again? What happens to bring on these episodes in which my skin cries out to be touched and my body longs for union, for completeness, for fulfillment? Union has to do with love and communication on many levels, not just at the physical level of the sexual act, even at its highest. Neither of my marriages had been a deep union, yet there had been a great deal of physical sexual activity. Though there had been a certain amount of "puppy" love in my first marriage, and a sincere desire on the part of my husband and me to reach each other emotionally, still we had never been able to mature enough individually or in our relationship to build the kind of mutual trust and openness which are the bases for something deeper. Though there were high moments when we felt very close, and the sex act was, as it should be, both natural and very beautiful, still, our needs caused us to use this expression of love as a way to *get* love rather than a way to *give* it.

In the second marriage, which was ill-fated from the beginning, two people who had more hate in their hearts than love used the sex act and their sexuality to destroy each other.

I had to admit that sex, therefore, was neither bad nor good in and of itself. Sex fell into much the same category as one's potential ability, one's intellect, one's imagination.

By this stage in my search for wholeness, I was well aware that all things were originally created for good and with a purpose. What good, then, was this sexual energy? What larger purpose did it have? What potential should it fulfill other than providing personal pleasure (which soon palls), progeny (which is, for many, an impossibility, and which value is now weakened by the threat of overpopulation), or the frosting on the cake of deepening relationships within marriage bonds? What use could it have for me, a single middle-aged woman, here and now?

At last my body was at peace, and blessed sleep soon enfolded it. I did not know it then, but what happened that night resulted in three goods: (1) The fact that I had found release by *moving outside myself* for an answer helped me see that this energy given to us as a gift of nature and grace is meant to be used in the service of love far beyond anything we can imagine at our present stage of human development on this globe. (2) That experience set me on an irreversible course to use this energy creatively—to disallow its using me, frustrating me, making me its slave. (3) It was the first opening to a whole new understanding of sex, personhood, and the spiritual life.

It took me time, effort, some embarrassment, and lots of work—but the release and freedom I gained far surpassed my wildest dreams—freedom and release which, I am convinced, would not be possible without the power of God's mercy and love. At fifty I have more energy than I had at thirty-five, and I attribute this largely to victory in channeling sexual energy by learning to love more people more fully without genital sex, and to my acceptance —joyful acceptance—of the single state of life.

Nature

My response to nature, or God's creation, has had a profound influence on my spiritual and creative life. As I look back in memory before 1961, life appears gray. I can't remember color at all, which seems strange since tests I took as early as 1945 indicated my color perceptivity ranged in the upper 3 percent of all persons tested. Still, it's true. Before spiritual awakening, the world was dull and gray just as I was dull and gray and just as I wore dull, gray dresses.

I seemed completely removed from nature. It was "out there," alien—or rather I was an alien to it. I had little interest in trees, flowers, grass—it all seemed so separated from me.

The first realization I had of my condition, which Dr. Elliott described as psychic death, was in the summer of 1962. I was at Pendle Hill, a Quaker community, where I had gone to learn more about the spiritual life and to do research, as well, on community life.

One breathless, hot, July day, when not a sigh was in the air, I sat on a cement step dejectedly considering the pros and cons of whether to move to New York City with the office and the Elliotts when they moved. I was in a blue funk. Why must my whole world fall apart just when I seem to be achieving a little stability and interest in life? Would I be able to get a job if I stayed in Cleveland? Nothing had materialized from the contacts I had made, and forty-three seemed to me a very dangerous age.

Wanting terribly to cry, I put my head on my knees in order to stem the flood of tears. Gradually I centered down emotionally, and for a few brief moments seemed as still as the motionless day. I made no effort at all. I simply was.

A slight breeze brushed by. I opened one eye and observed a miracle. One slender blade of grass, very fresh, very green, and very vibrant, arched itself toward me. My entire being seemed to rush to meet it in total response. My body tingled, and joy washed over and through me—a quiet joy which desired nothing more than to respond fully to that beautiful blade of grass. Here was another evidence of God's love and care for us, his children. This dancing, bending, beckoning blade of grass God had created, and it was a miracle! My response, too, was a miracle. Joy was a miracle—a true gift of grace.

The newfound joy receded only slightly when the dinner bell rang and I moved on. A remnant of the joy remained all day.

Later in the afternoon I was walking beside a wide, open field on the other side of which was a thick stand of trees. I was contemplating God's love and mercy, immersing myself once again in the wonder of the acts of a God who expresses his concern and care in so many ways. Why are we so slow to comprehend? I wondered.

A whirring near the trees caught my attention. I stopped to

listen. The soft sound took on a muted staccato beat and finally a fullness like the tramping of many armies. The marchers, I felt, had started before the beginning of time and would go on till the end of time. At first I wondered if they were the armies of war, but they did not seem like determined, heavy, or angry footsteps. I quieted myself and listened more intently. The pasture grass had come alive in a very specific manner—the individual blades were dressed in green diamonds which glistened in the sun, and they were dancing sprightly little jigs.

But the marching continued, and in the silent stillness I "knew" that those feet were the feet of the lonely, the blind, the deaf, the hungry, the lame, and the lost. I also knew irrevocably that I had a responsibility to help make their steps dance like the blades of grass—in celebrative abandonment and joy.

Since that day I have recognized that nature, too, is used by God to help us come into the light of life here and now. Each new deepening experience has given me a deepening appreciation for God's world. I moved from alienation through the wonderment of awakening to a deeper cosmic reality and a sense of true mission in one day—a day which in the timelessness of God's presence seemed like eternity.

Through the years since that time I have moved from grays to light and color; from light and color in all natural phenomena to color and sparkle; next, to color, vibrancy, shape, and form; then, color began to appear in subtle places one would not usually look. Nature and I seem to have merged; my environment is not outside me but is an indispensable part of me. We are one.

Creative potential: the imagination. The first year of this new life had been taken up with: (1) learning to accept the love of my newfound friends; (2) learning to trust them and their love; (3) separating my own desires, wishes, feelings from the expectations others had of me; (4) learning to choose the responses I would make rather than reacting impulsively to persons and situations; (5) learning to live in the present moment rather than in past experiences.

Now awareness was dawning that my frustration was due in large part to not using my full potential, not loving others, and having little respect for myself. About this time I received a letter:

Dear Mrs. Payne:

Toynbee has said that when a civilization comes to a time of troubles such as we are now in, individuals here and there turn from the outer world of political and social chaos to the inner world where they come upon the vision of a new way of life. Returning to the outer world, they form the nucleus of a creative minority through which that civilization may find renewal.

We, here at _____, are on an experiment designed to help teach us how the conscious and the unconscious can be enabled to work together, how we can develop the inward eye, the inward ear, the inward understanding in such a way that we can deal with others with unshockable interest and noncensuring concern.

As a people, we seem to have become willfully indifferent to the depths of other persons and disdainful of our own selves. Communication has broken down among us. We will learn how to listen to the depths of ourselves, our neighbor, and God in order to learn to relate to self and others in a deeper, more meaningful manner.

We hope also to revive the creative imagination of everyone who joins the search with us for the purpose of learning to fulfill our true potential.

Sincerely,

_____

This "experiment in learning to live again" seemed exactly the answer to my search, and so I signed up for a series of six weekends. We were asked to come to these sessions with an open mind, an expectant attitude, and a willingness to be honest. The same people participated during all six sessions. Each person was asked to make a commitment to the group not to be absent, the purpose being threefold: (1) to provide, in the act of commitment itself, a growth experience; (2) to maintain group unity and continuity in growth; and (3) to foster among us the growth of trust, trust being essential to spiritual growth.

This course was a splendid aid in helping bring together some of the elements of my personal search. We twenty-five human beings had a rare opportunity to share together in work, play, study, dialogue, prayer, silence, and creative pursuits. We discussed and studied fairy tales, Bible stories, myths, legends, symbolism, and our dreams. Most of us did learn to listen. And for me the discoveries I made during the creative projects and the listening sessions were most valuable at that stage of my life.

Half the creative period was taken up with art and the other with writing. We were always asked to meditate on something before starting to create: some particular object or arrangement of objects, a poem, dream, painting, or music. The reflective period was for the purpose of stopping the thinking machine so that unconscious material could surface. "Each of us has an indestructible vein of Life. We touch Life direct, from childhood to adulthood. Beneath the layers of staleness, the artist child is still alive in us. Our business is to allow this child to grow . . . ; we must hold back the critics in ourselves until we have given this inner child a chance," * was the premise. Another was: "Adults look enviously at children, wishing for that visible joy in play, that casualness, that spontaneity. Through the art group they may re-find this lost part of themselves. If not for their own sakes, adults should make the attempt for the sake of the children around them." †

The learning experience of that first art session continues to grow each time I reflect upon it. We stood around that table like sticks with smiles on them. Personally, I felt like a lump of dried clay. The embarrassment of doing anything of an artistic nature

---

* From "A Sense of Living" by Mildred Tonge, p. 21, Pendle Hill Pamphlet No. 79, copyright 1954 by Pendle Hill, Wallingford, Pa. 19086.

† *Ibid.,* p. 27.

before others was severe. I was unnerved at the thought of exposing my inadequacies and lack of talent.

Most of us stood looking at the table, avoiding one another's glance. The leader suggested that we look at the ink bottles, taking time to "exercise the seeing" so that we could get in touch once again with the sense of sight, so that the eyes could be reborn.

Next she asked us to drop colored ink on a large piece of white paper, to take deep breaths and blow as hard as possible, and to *feel* what we were doing. There were varying degrees of unwillingness to perform this childish exercise. I, for one, wanted no part in it. How timidly I approached the first breath, which originated no farther back than my throat. I was worried about how the others would see me, how ridiculous I must look, what a mess I was going to make of the white paper. As we were goaded to blow harder and harder, I felt a tremendous release of tension and, later, a sense of exhilaration. The beautiful patterns the colors made without regard to technique helped me in later sessions not to be concerned about becoming a great artist. This was not the point. The point was *to learn to feel again,* to awaken one's awareness and open one's pores to the world. The exercise also helped open us to one another. We had entered into an embarrassing situation, passed through it, and come out closer in understanding. Our masks had slipped just a tiny bit. We didn't have to be perfect (paint a pretty picture or act in some particular way) in order to be accepted.

I had a very personal experience of my own deep hostility during this exercise. In the middle of one of my hardest blows I began to think about blowing all my angers away. By the time the exercise was complete I felt a new sense of release.

This and the other projects in art expression (working in clay, finger painting, making collages) opened me to a whole new world of awareness, beauty, and self-knowledge, and provided me with yet another way to worship God and celebrate life. These and the writing sessions were, for me, the most fruitful experiences of the growth-group seminars, since they represented the portion of my life most neglected.

One weekend, during a period when anger and guilt seemed to be the most prominent occupations of my mind and nothing—prayer, discussion, meditation—seemed to help, our leader placed a lovely shell with mother-of-pearl interior in the center of a low coffee table. Beside the shell she placed a graceful piece of driftwood upon which was perched a tiny toy gull, set for flight.

As I reflected on this still life I recognized that *I* was still only partially in flight. I recalled a time at the seashore when I had been trying to run away from a spell of loneliness, and I wrote:

I walked along the white sand, and the jewels of the sea surrounded me—shells of lustrous beauty polished by the surfing of the sea. But look!—a special gem swept up there. Was this gift for me?

All life seems contained here in this magic moment. The majesty of the white-capped sea, spellbinding, awakening one to awe and wonder. Yet see the lonely driftwood flung upon the sand, worn by time and discarded by the elements. But no! not completely—for just now I see a white-winged gull choose this lonely piece to land upon.

Loneliness and longing
fulfilled by the surging and beating—
life and death,
jewels and deadwood,
stillness and vibrant life,
light and dark,
yearning and joy,
me and thee.

In a few brief moments it became clear that the so-called negatives of life from which we try to flee may be the very ingredients necessary for growth. Rather than wallow in the muck of self-pity and anger, we must use them to move toward love and confidence. The anger is a goad to love.

On another weekend, when we congregated for our writing session, we found dozens of articles from which we could choose for reflection. Among these were such things as a rag doll, a cream pitcher, jewelry, children's toys, a pair of mittens, several smooth stones. My eyes fell on two lovely, lithe African statues—one man, one woman. The woman was carrying a heavily laden basket on her head; the man was beating a drum. I felt I could hear those drums and feel the rhythm of the dark man who has such power and grace. I wrote:

> O black bodies
>   lithe and beautiful,
>   supple and graceful;
>   with dignity you bear your load
>   —your cross.
>   With nobility you seek your freedom.
> What trials and pains you have to bear;
> Your people's joyous hearts—
>   are they a fruit of the pain?
> We call you primitive
>   but hate you because
>   *we have less inner freedom than you—*
>   *and less pain—*
>   *and less joy.*
> We despise your beautiful, bronzed bodies
>   because ours are so pale and
>   it's so much trouble for us to get ours to have
>   that burnished glow.
>   But
>   Oh! we try!
> We debase your efforts to become civilized and say you
>   aren't up to it,
>   when we actually fear

our own abilities,
our own selves.
Why will we not accept you as our brothers
and heal our personal
and national wounds?
Why must we fight against you?
  Probably because
    we buck all of life,
    all God would pour out on us
    —even our shadow selves.
Oh! to be able to flow and bend and dance to life!

The response to these statues had been so immediate I did not analyze what had occurred within me until the exercise was complete. For several months I had been struggling with my crippling prejudices concerning my black sisters and brothers. The barriers between us were a source of great pain to me, but my own feelings were a greater source of pain.

During these creative projects three crippling facets of my character were exposed: (1) perfectionism, (2) an almost complete loss of sensitivity of touch, and (3) what appeared to be death of the imagination. These three added up to a dogmatic and rigid approach to life which left little room for flexibility, give and take, gratitude and joy.

These projects also taught me a positive and productive lesson about how creativity comes about. The seeking, searching, reading, praying, and talking are necessary ingredients to finding answers. On the other hand, silence, art, writing, meditation, and developing as fully as possible all the senses help us find more adequate answers.

A New Self

The life-to-death spiral went downward all the way. Anger turned to self-pity and guilt, which resulted in negative forms of social action: sometimes an overt burst of anger, other times repression. Sometimes I actually was rejected, but more often than not my own lack of identity and my guilt feelings caused me to feel I was rejected when in reality this was not the case. I would withdraw to lick my wounds and repress my anger, and the cycle would start over again with a new load of fear and feelings of inadequacy. It bore a downward thrust because at each cycle I became more concerned about my own feelings and hurts; this narrowed my horizon and social milieu until at last I was in the proverbial hell of living only for myself. As Carol Linder King put it, "Hell is the kind of anguish a man inflicts upon himself. It is the eternal isolation of the soul who rejects love. It is the eternal darkness of the soul who shuts out the light. Hell is self-deception." * This kind of hell not only rejects love but refuses to face its angers so that it *can* love.

My deception wore many masks, but one of the most successful was the generous use of money and gifts, especially with my family. The gifts I showered on others helped me deceive myself into believing I was really quite altruistic and outgoing, even loving. It was a lie, and my body and soul bore the brunt of that lie.

Another mask was busyness. It took me a long time to recognize several aspects of busyness that were keeping me in my prison: (1) Working long hours overtime was a manifestation not of a deep desire to help my boss, even though that was a factor, but of fear that I would not measure up to expectations—his or my own. (2) My extracurricular activities were not resulting in friendships with others or in zest for life. Rather, they were an excuse not to be alone to face myself or the boredom and loneliness which waited to pounce upon me the moment I entered my apartment. (3) The fact that other people complimented me for all I was doing created a web from which I seemed powerless to extricate myself. Their compliments made me feel good for a

---

* Carol Linder King, "An Epitaph for Lost Souls," *United Church Herald* (March 1967).

short while, just enough so that when I considered quitting in order to do something more worthwhile and meaningful, I would feel guilty and ungrateful. In my experience, the church and churchy people are both the spiders and flies in this kind of drama. The only way to deal with it within the system is to get busier and busier, but the only way *really* to deal with it is to face the reality of what is happening and not happening; to face one's own needs and motivations.

I discovered that often when I ripped off one mask it was only to find another beneath, and another and another. But each one ripped off was a liberation from bondage, and well worth the effort.

The death-to-birth process reversed the spiral. In the pit of hell certain persons reached down in trust and love. For me it was important that these persons first loved God and were mature enough to have a healthy regard for their own personhood. When the love had been sustained long enough for my wounded ego to begin to trust, I was able to express verbally my anger and frustration. With a little of the volcanic steam released, I could look at some of the reasons for the anger, and thus the guilt was lessened. As the guilt and anger were reduced there was less need for self-pity. I became a little more outgoing and lovable, and persons were not so easily threatened by me. Soon I made more friends with whom I could be open—in addition to those who had come into the pit after me. Openness led to releasing more anger in more productive and socially acceptable ways. As I gave up self-pity I was able more and more to look outside myself. Awareness and compassion gradually increased. The spiral is still opening out as I open myself to more of what life has to offer—as I say YES to life.

Each step of the opening-out process demanded a sacrifice, a death, and what felt like a rebirth. Always there was fear and ultimately a leap of faith which made it seem for a while that nothing was certain. Sometimes, though not always, reactions and attitudes I had thought long dead revived. Anger and fear have had the most frequent reruns: fear to move into the unknown; fear that once again I would be left on the high, lone rock of lovelessness; anger at myself for being so resistant to change and so slow to respond and so clumsy when I finally did respond.

But sacrifice and death were only one side of the coin. Each ring of the spiral has moved up and out, releasing energy and allowing in more and more light, air, peace, and joy. I came to know myself, other people, and God each time at greater depth; music and art became more meaningful; prejudices fell away, leaving me free to love former "enemies"; deep fatigue disappeared, my skin and eyes became clearer, my health robust and abundant, my body clean where it once felt dirty—my ally in witness and service where once I looked on it as an ugly alien. I seemed to become more immersed in the cosmos itself; the wind, trees, grass, and flowers; noises of the city, sea, sky, and land in some mystical manner seemed almost to become an extension of my own skin. My self became less and less a prison. The death of destructive attitudes through recognition, repentance, confession, and restitution had to take place before the new could come into being.

Once the self was released from its bondages of guilt, fear, and anger, I was freed to do many things I had formerly thought impossible. At forty-five years of age I entered seminary against the advice of many professional people who felt I was too old. Later I began to paint and to have a deepening appreciation for all forms of art. Gradually I was enabled to become creatively involved in the lives of others—to give and accept love and help and attention because I now felt acceptable. Next I discovered a satisfying vocation which later turned into a cause to which I could give myself wholeheartedly.

This, then, is not the end of the story—but the beginning.

NOTES

Introduction

1. "Our group" and "singler" here and elsewhere mean middle-aged (thirty-fifty-five) single women, the primary target of this book.

Chapter 4   Woman's Image

1. M. D. Hugen, *The Church's Ministry to the Older Unmarried* (Grand Rapids, Mich.: Eerdmans, 1959), p. 25. Used by permission.

2. Madeleine Barot, *Cooperation of Men and Women in Church, Family, and Society* (Department on Cooperation of Men and Women in the Church, Family, and Society, World Council of Churches, 1964), p. 6.

3. Hugen, *op. cit.*, p. 64.

4. *Ibid.*

5. © 1966 by The New York Times Company. Reprinted by permission.

6. Hugen, *op. cit.*, p. 34.

7. *Ibid.*, p. 40.

8. *Ibid.*, p. vii.

9. From *Religious Pathology and Christian Faith*, by James E. Loder. The Westminster Press. Copyright © 1966, W. L. Jenkins. Used by permission.

10. For a discussion of homosexuality, see *The Same Sex: An Appraisal of Homosexuality*, ed. Ralph W. Weltge (Philadelphia: Pilgrim Press, 1969). Also see Leonard Hodgson, *Sex and Christian Freedom: An Enquiry* (London: SCM Press, 1967).

11. I myself think of masturbation as a self-centered indulgence. I qualify my statement by admitting that others may find it not an enervating introversion but a simple release of tension. Recent research on this subject should make us all less dogmatic. However, I must testify here to the creative possibilities in abstinence.

12. From W. R. Johnson, *Masturbation*, SIECUS Study Guide # 3, p. 8, New York: Sex Information & Education Council of the U. S., revised October 1968.

13. *Saturday Evening Post*, Vol. 240, No. 2 (January 28, 1967).

Chapter 6   The Physical Life

1. *Ripon College Alumnus* (February 1968).

2. *Ibid.*

3. From *Beyond Birth Control* by Sidney Cornelia Callahan, © Sheed & Ward, Inc., 1968, p. 66.

4. *Ibid.*, p. 67.

Chapter 7   Employment

1. *Time*, Vol. 91, No. 12 (March 23, 1968).

2. J. C. Wynn (ed.), *Sex, Family, and Society in Theological Focus* (New York: Association Press, 1966), p. 176,

Chapter 9   Participation

1. C. G. Jung, *Modern Man in Search of a Soul,* trans. W. S. Dell and Cary F. Baynes (New York: Harcourt, Brace & Co., 1933), pp. 108-9. Used by permission of Harcourt, Brace & World.

2. *Report of the Committee on Education of the President's Commission on the Status of Women* (October 1963), U. S. Government Printing Office, Washington, D.C. 20402, p. 4.

3. *Ibid.,* pp. 6-7.

4. Paraphrased from Pearl S. Buck, *Children for Adoption* (New York: Random House, 1964), pp. 126-27.

5. Jack Shepherd, "Miracle on 12th Street," *United Church Herald,* Vol. 11, No. 7 (July 1968), pp. 15-16.

6. Kirkridge, Bangor, Pennsylvania 18013.

7. Emmaus House, 141 East 116th Street, New York, New York 10029.

8. Ann Ryan, "New Communities of Men and Women," p. 4. Miss Ryan's address is 704 East Pyron Street, San Antonio, Texas 78214. Write for further information.

9. The Ecumenical Institute, 3444 Congress Parkway, Chicago, Illinois 60624.

10. Newman Cryer, "Laboratory for Tomorrow's Church," *Together* (March 1966).

11. Reba Place Fellowship, 727 Reba Place, Evanston, Illinois 60202.

12. Jane Bishop, "Apple Farm," *The Church Woman* (February 1967), p. 19.

13. *Ibid.,* p. 20.

14. Martha S. Harre, "The Oil of Joy for Mourning."

15. Theo, Inc., 11609 Frankstown Road, Pittsburgh, Pennsylvania 15235.

16. Stephen C. Rose, "The New Urban Congregation: From Renewal to Resistance," *Renewal* (January–February 1968), p. 9.

17. Church Women United, Eighth Floor, 475 Riverside Drive, New York, New York 10027.

18. *On Our Way Together,* Church Women United booklet on resources, program, guidelines (National Council of Churches, 1968), p. 42.

19. *Ibid.,* p. 27.

20. *Ibid.,* p. 44.

21. Charles Davis, "The Modern Parish: A Conference Paper," *Guide* # 211 (October 1966), p. 8.

RESOURCES

ACHTEMEIER, ELIZABETH. *The Feminine Crisis in Christian Faith.* Nashville, Tenn.: Abingdon Press, 1965. The author brings to light some of the weaknesses in the religious beliefs and activities of the middle-class American woman. After her analysis of the prevailing situation she provides an interpretation of woman's true religious role based on a more adequate biblical understanding and expressed in the idea that the Christian life can be lived only in community with others on the basis of a sufficient knowledge of God. A married woman, she centers her theme on the family; but there are good ideas here for any woman.

American Women: Report of the President's Commission on the Status of Women. Washington, D.C.: Superintendent of Documents, 1963. Reports of committees on civil and political rights, education, federal employment, home and community, private employment, protective labor legislation, social insurance, and taxes. Also included are excellent charts and statistics. Obtainable from the Women's Bureau of the Department of Labor, or purchasable from the Superintendent of Documents, Washington.

Are You Nobody? Richmond, Va.: John Knox Press, 1966. Essays by Paul Tournier, Viktor E. Frankl, Harry Levinson, Helmut Thielicke, Paul Lehmann, and Samuel H. Miller deal with the question "Are you a nobody, a thing, or a person?"

ARNOLD, F. X. *Woman and Man, Their Nature and Mission.* Translated by Rosaleen Brennan. New York: Herder & Herder, 1963. Father Arnold sees woman as the providential force for preserving man from the destructive powers unleashed by his technological bent. He sees woman's achievement as both social and spiritual.

BEARD, MARY. *Woman as Force in History: A Study in Traditions and Realities.* New York: Macmillan, 1946. This book has an excellent bibliography. It deals with contributions of women throughout the history of the Western world.

BEAUVOIR, SIMONE DE. *The Second Sex,* ed. and trans. by H. M. Parshley. New York: Knopf, 1953; Bantam, 1961. Controversial, original, reckless, penetrating. Her section on history is suggestive and shows encyclopedic knowledge. Her interpretation is somewhat slanted toward the idea that men have kept women ignorant and disenfranchised for their own purposes. The author explores in depth the female sexual, social, and cultural life from childhood through menopause, culminating in a forecast of woman's potential in tomorrow's world.

BERNARD, JESSIE. *Academic Women.* University Park, Pa.: The Pennsylvania State University Press, 1964. The author does not allow her own values to distort the logic of evidence. She seeks to account for the decline since 1930 in the proportion of academic personnel who are women. She examines differences in career patterns and achievements of men and women.

BIRD, CAROLINE. *Born Female: The High Cost of Keeping Women Down.* New York: David McKay Co., 1968. This book is directed largely to the working woman. Mrs. Bird helps us to see that in keeping women down, men have created a great social and economic waste which is morally wrong: women's talents are hidden and destroyed in a system which oppresses them. (Women are also guilty in having allowed this to happen.) But things are changing due to higher education for adults, the demand for technological skills and executive talent, and the Pill, which gives women more freedom for self-determination.

BLISS, KATHLEEN. *Service and Status of Women in the Church.* London: SCM Press, 1953. A comparative study of Protestant churches throughout the world. It stresses three areas especially—professional, volunteer, and executive, policy-making positions for women. Factual.

BORROMEO, SISTER M. CHARLES (ed.). *The New Nuns.* New York: New American Library, 1967. A symposium which looks to better ways to harness the energy and potential of nuns in order that they can work in more socially relevant ways for the betterment of our world. These nuns tell what they think of virginity, Freud, protest movements, convent life, Vatican II, the coif and veil, and why they want to get into the revolutions of the twentieth century.

BURNS, ELIZABETH. *The Late Liz: The Autobiography of an Expagan.* New York: Appleton-Century-Crofts, 1957. A moving story of one woman's conversion.

BUYTENDIJK, F. J. J. *Woman: A Contemporary View.* Translated by Denis J. Barrett. New York: Association Press; Glen Rock, N.J.: Newman Press, 1968. A deep, probing, affectionate picture of modern woman: how she talks, laughs, moves, reacts to other women and to men. Buytendijk wants woman to have a higher estimation of herself as a womanly, free, complete human being. He sees woman as mystery, abyss, mother, and body. An excellent book.

CARRÉ, A. M. (ed.). *The Vocation of the Single Woman: A Symposium of Views and Testimonies.* Translated by Una Morrissy. New York: P. J. Kenedy & Sons, 1960. These pieces concern the celibate life. Both the dangers and the opportunities are discussed.

CASSARA, BEVERLY BENNER (ed.). *American Women: The Changing Image.* Boston: Beacon Press, 1962. Forthright ideas expressed by eleven distinguished women concerning the struggle for women's rights. The contributors are by no means unanimous in their opinions. The book raises many questions on the role of American women, offers some answers, and challenges all to give thought to how educated women can best fulfill their responsibilities in an increasingly complex world.

CROOK, MARGARET BRACKENBURY. *Women and Religion.* Boston: Beacon Press, 1965. The author traces the loss of status and function of women in the three great religious groups stemming from the lands and books of the Bible—Judaism, Christianity, and Islam—to present-day Protestantism. The author appeals to men and women alike to utilize women's innate life-conserving capacities and intuitive insights to meet the needs of today. She says, "Women have a heritage in religion to regain, develop, and carry forward."

Daedalus, Journal of the American Academy of Arts and Sciences (Spring 1964). A very important collection of articles for any-one interested in the changing roles of women. Topics include: "Working Women," "Two Generations," "Reflections on Womanhood," and other pertinent subjects.

DANIÉLOU, JEAN. *Prayer as a Political Problem,* ed. and trans. by J. R. Kirwan. New York: Sheed & Ward, 1967. This book faces the issue: "There can be no radical division between civilization and what belongs to the interior being of man; there must be a dialogue between prayer and the pursuit and realization of public policy."

LANGDON-DAVIES, JOHN. *A Short History of Women.* New York: Viking Press, 1927. Useful because of its outline form.

DEUTSCH, HELENE. *The Psychology of Women: A Psychoanalytic Interpretation.* New York: Grune & Stratton, 1944–1945. Vol-ume I: Girlhood; Volume II: Motherhood. A complete and erudite picture of the psychological life of the "normal" woman in our society with pathological material used only to high-light. Rather heavy, but worth it.

DEUAUX, ANDRE. *Teilhard and Womanhood.* Translated by P. J. Oligny, O.F.M. and M. D. Meilach, O.F.M. Deus Books; New York: Paulist Press, 1968. A brief study which contains direct quotes from Teilhard's writings as well as from his letters and reactions to women he knew. Stresses modern woman's vocation to the world in not only bearing children but in bearing love.

DINGWALL, ERIC JOHN. *The American Woman: A Historical Study.* London: Gerald Duckworth & Co., 1956. Dr. Dingwall traces the development of the American woman from colonial days to the present (1956). As the dust jacket says: "In the view of this author, the conflict in the soul of many American women is primarily a sexual conflict, connected with the much-heralded American Way of Life, where men are supreme in business and women in society."

Dodd, C. H. *Christ and the New Humanity.* Philadelphia: Fortress Press, 1965. Deals with both the "personal and corporate Christian witness as a leaven in human society" and the concept that the Christian ethic is of the spirit.

Dumas, Francine. *Man and Woman: Similarity and Difference.* Geneva, Switzerland: World Council of Churches, 1966. Very important and balanced statement regarding masculine and feminine identity, covering psychological, sociological, cultural, theological insights. Marriage and family oriented.

Erikson, Erik H. *Identity and the Life Cycle.* New York: International Universities Press, 1959. (*Psychological Issues,* Volume I, Number 1, Monograph 1.) The author deals with ego development, growth, and crises of the healthy personality, and the problem of ego identity.

————. *Insight and Responsibility.* New York: W. W. Norton & Co., 1964. Discusses the ethical implications of psychoanalytic insight and the responsibilities that each generation of men has for all succeeding generations. Inner conflict and geographical uprootedness and the human life cycle are some of the matters Erikson deals with in this collection of six lectures.

Frankl, Viktor E. *Man's Search for Meaning.* Translated by Ilse Lasch. New York: Washington Square Press, 1963. Dr. Frankl describes his harrowing years in Nazi prison camps during which he developed Logotherapy, a concept which adds a new dimension to the basic theories of modern psychology. Helps us understand our times as well as ourselves.

Friedan, Betty. *The Feminine Mystique.* New York: W. W. Norton & Co., 1963. A well-documented book which explores the mystique of woman as housewife-mother. Important to all women who wish to understand the images perpetuated by elements of modern society, many of which need changing.

Gross, Irma H. (ed.). *Potentialities of Women in the Middle*

Years. East Lansing, Mich.: Michigan State University Press, 1956. The authors discuss the "task" of adult women as "intellectual and emotional expansion." An outgrowth of a symposium conducted by the school of home economics at Michigan State University.

HUGEN, M. D. *The Church's Ministry to the Older Unmarried.* Grand Rapids, Mich.: Eerdmans, 1959. The author addresses the social problem, personal problems, and theological foundations of the older unmarried person and expresses concern that the church and society come to grips with the fact that the middle-aged single person is mistreated in our culture. I recommend this book highly.

JOURARD, SIDNEY M. *The Transparent Self: Self-Disclosure and Well-Being.* Princeton, N.J.: D. Van Nostrand Co., 1964. Professor Jourard maintains that lack of openness and honesty all too often results in sickness, misunderstanding, and alienation of self. "Spirit" is important to Professor Jourard's theme.

KENT, PATRICIA. *An American Woman and Alcohol.* New York: Holt, Rinehart & Winston, 1967. Patricia Kent discusses the woman alcoholic herself, her family, her job, the men in her life, her appearance, and the "ways out." Miss Kent also includes a chapter on escape from pills—pep pills, pain pills, and the false paradise of "simple" (nonprescription) drugs.

LINDBERGH, ANNE MORROW. *Gift from the Sea.* New York: Pantheon, 1955. An aesthetically pleasing analysis of modern woman's need for an inner core to give her stability amidst today's restlessness and unending demands. Useful for a greater understanding of the need and values of the inner life or for devotional material.

LOOMIS, EARL A. *The Self in Pilgrimage.* New York: Harper & Row, 1960. Dr. Loomis believes that the self cannot be understood apart from religion and psychology combined. In this book he deals in a new way with the religious dimensions of selfhood and with the relation of the self to the religious community of grace.

MASLOW, ABRAHAM H. *Toward a Psychology of Being*. Insight Books; Princeton, N.J.: D. Van Nostrand Co., 1962. The author's theory that psychology as a science can "help in positive human fulfillment" by "enlarging and deepening of the conception of its nature, its goals, and its methods is classically presented. He writes affirmatively concerning growth, motivation, cognition, creativeness, values, and future tasks.

MAY, ROLLO. *Man's Search for Himself*. New York: W. W. Norton & Co., 1953. Highly recommended. It is a forthright and highly imaginative study of the contemporary predicament. Dr. May helps us to see how we can "find a center of strength within ourselves to face and conquer the insecurities of this troubled age."

MAY, WILLIAM P. *A Catalogue of Sins: A Contemporary Examination of Christian Conscience*. New York: Holt, Rinehart & Winston, 1967. "This book is about the several sins rather than the sinfulness of man," and the author provides keen insight without sentimentalism, moralism, legalism, and abstractions into the underlying reality from which sins derive.

MONTAGU, ASHLEY. *The Natural Superiority of Women*. New York: Macmillan, 1952. A polemical marshaling of the data on one side of a scholarly anthropological debate. Mr. Montagu risked the wrath of his own sex in writing this book, but he says of it, "The plea of this book is for more mutual love and understanding and complete social equality of the sexes."

MOULE, C. F. D. *The Meaning of Hope: A Biblical Exposition with Concordance*. Facet Books; Philadelphia: Fortress Press, 1953. Biblical hope is more than a wish. Dr. Moule helps us see hope as realistic, moral, trustful, and walking hand in hand with forgiveness.

NYBERG, KATHLEEN NEILL. *The New Eve: A Feminine Look at Christian Style*. Nashville, Tenn.: Abingdon Press, 1967. Another book for the married woman, but one that is witty and full of wisdom. It will help all women better understand a passable Christian life-style for our present age.

OLDHAM, J. H. *Florence Allshorn.* New York: Harper & Bros.,
1952. The biography of a great and saintly missionary who built
the community of St. Julian's for the rehabilitation of mis-
sionaries. A warm, moving story.

PARKER, ELIZABETH. *The Seven Ages of Woman,* ed. Evelyn Brock.
Baltimore, Md.: Johns Hopkins Press, 1960. A remarkably
comprehensive, detailed guide to the phases of woman's life:
childhood and the strictly feminine problems of young girls,
the onset of maturity, physical and emotional maturation, marriage and the ideals of marriage, conception and the miracle of
birth, menopause, the later years.

PRICE, EUGENIA. *A Woman's Choice: Living Through Your
Problems from Confusion to Peace.* Grand Rapids, Mich.:
Zondervan, 1962. The author says, "This is her [a woman's]
choice. . . . We can *live through* our problems, from confusion to peace, or we can bumble along taking the jolts which
inevitably follow a life guided only by the often stormy and
reckless winds of our emotions." Love can overcome the con-
fusions which result from doubt, ingratitude, ignorance, darkness, extremism, problems in relationships, and so forth.

RUITENBEEK, HENDRICK M. *The Male Myth.* New York: Dell,
1967. Men too are in transition and need to find a new identity.

RYRIE, CHARLES C. *The Place of Women in the Church.* New
York: Macmillan, 1958. Traces the history of the place of
women in the church from ancient Greece to the apostolic age
with many biblical references.

SCHUTZ, WILLIAM C. *Joy: Expanding Human Awareness.* New
York: Grove Press, 1967. As the dust jacket says, "This book
describes revolutionary new techniques for preserving one's
identity amid the pressures of mass society. . . . Through
group thinking, talking, touching, hugging, and acting out
life-situations, one can transform suspicion into trust, hostility
into love, and dullness into awareness."

SNYDER, ROSS. *On Becoming Human: Discovering Yourself and
Your Life World.* Nashville, Tenn.: Abingdon Press, 1967. Life

is meant to be lived and each of us is a center of aliveness for this author. He wastes no words.

STENDAHL, KRISTER. *The Bible and the Role of Women.* Biblical Series; Philadelphia: Fortress Press, 1966. Of particular value to women who are interested in ordination of women in the church.

STERN, KARL. *The Flight from Woman.* New York: Farrar, Straus & Giroux, 1965. The polarity of the sexes is important to this author. He contends that the masculine tenor of our society is dehumanizing to women and is creating a world impoverished of womanly values.

THURIAN, MAX. *Marriage and Celibacy.* Translated by Norma Emerton. London: SCM Press, 1959. Or see Alec L. Allenson, Naperville, Ill. The central purpose of this book is "to interpret the Word of God on the subject of marriage and celibacy in an ecumenical spirit . . . seeking . . . to express the truth of the gospel." The author maintains that "When the vocation of celibacy is undervalued, so is that of marriage." Excellent.

―――. *Mary, Mother of All Christians.* Translated by Neville B. Cryer. New York: Herder & Herder, 1964. This book will help both Catholic and Protestant women to understand the meaning of the biblical texts that relate to the life of the virgin Mary. This is essentially a spiritual theology of Mary which explores in a biblical setting the meaning of Mary's virginity and motherhood.

TOURNIER, PAUL. *Escape from Loneliness.* Translated by John S. Gilmour. Philadelphia: Westminster Press, 1961, Highly recommended. Loneliness is the malady of the age, believes Dr. Tournier, and this malady is due to our spirit of competition, our spirit of independence, our possessiveness. The corrective is a spirit of fellowship.

―――. *The Meaning of Persons.* Translated by Edwin Hudson. New York: Harcourt, Brace & World, 1957. Dr. Tournier believes that the true meaning of a person cannot be divorced from the biblical perspective or from his feelings about religion.

VAN DER POST, LAURENS. *Venture to the Interior*. New York: William Morrow & Co., 1951. A great personal adventure story which combines true narrative with philosophical comment, and a moving spiritual adventure.

WINTER, GIBSON. *Love and Conflict: New Patterns in Family Life*. Garden City, N.Y.: Doubleday, 1958. Another book for the family. This book will be useful to the single woman for its clear, realistic examination of the pitfalls brought about by the pressures of the lonely crowd and organization men, which have had their effects on the entire society.

Women: Pro & Con. Mount Vernon, N.Y.: Peter Pauper Press, 1958. A selection of remarks made by famous men concerning women.